Classic
Dances
of the Orient

CLASSIC DANCES
of the ORIENT

Xenia Zarina

CROWN PUBLISHERS, INC., NEW YORK

All photographs are from the author's own collection, except where
otherwise indicated in the captions. Indian and Javanese hand and
foot positions are credited to Philippe Jardel.

To My Revered Teachers
Chandrasen Pillai, Tanjore, India
Kumar Jayakar, Bombay, India
Kunying Natakanuraksa, Directress of the Royal Siamese Ballet,
Bangkok, Thailand
Princess Say Sang Van, Phnom Penh, Cambodia
Pangeran Tedjokoesoemo, Djokjakarta, Java
Ida Bagoes Rai Nyoman Gria, Sanoer, Bali
Bjoman Kaler, Denpasar, Bali
Matsumoto Koshiro, Japan's great Kabuki actor
who graciously and patiently initiated me into their great dance art.

Foreword

IN ALL CIVILIZATIONS stage, dance, and ballet form the quintessence of a long tradition of cultural refinement. Indian dance can look back on a continuous tradition as far as the third millennium B.C., of which the figure of a dancing girl excavated at Mohenjo Daro is evidence.

In the Golden Age of Indian civilization under the Imperial Guptas, Indian dance assumed its classic form and its textbook from one of the ancient Hindu books of sacred writing, the *Natya Sastra* of Bharata Muni. But, though the *Natya Sastra* has been adhered to faithfully, it was open also to many subtle interpretations. The innumerable statues and reliefs of dancing girls on the temple façades of medieval India reveal many dance styles which have since disappeared—soft and gliding, rugged and angular —and contact with the Moslem world added more types, especially the rapid rotating movements of the North Indian nautches.

During classic and medieval times, Indian civilization conquered the whole of Southeastern Asia and strongly influenced the Far East. Indian dance is still a living tradition in Greater India—Ceylon, Burma, Thailand, Cambodia, Java, and Bali. But like the visual arts and music of these countries, their dances show considerable differences from those of India proper, differences which go back partly to social vicissitudes of the colonial kingdoms, partly to the influence of the original traditions of the Khmers, Thai, and Malays, and partly to the respective earlier stages of the Indian dance from which these various styles branched off. It can be safely asserted that the dances of Greater India in many cases preserve the classical Indian tradition better than those schools in India proper which at present are regarded as the authoritative guardians of a rich and brilliant past. Bharat Natyam is derived from the Vijayanagar, Chola, and Pallava traditions, but it is the Javanese Serimpi that still breathes the spirit of Gupta art broken only slightly through a Malay medium.

And yet what a wealth of local reinterpretation mirroring the special ideals of each individual cultural group! There are the beauty of the Indonesian dances, doll-like, similar to the Wayang figures moved by wooden or horn sticks; the dances inspirited by the magic possession of Balinese religiosity with its fusion of Saiva, Tantric-Buddhist, and Malay shamanistic experiences; the dances stylized into a series of perfect lineal pictures in the ceremonious Bedoyos and Serimpis of Surakarta and Djok-jakarta; the pomp of the ancient Khmer dances now surviving in the petrified fairyland of Apsarases at Angkor Vat, Angkor Thom, the Bayon, and Banteai Chmar; and the present-day Cambodian and Thai classic dances. All these reflect the old Gupta tradition.

In the Far East, Indian dance became known, together with Buddhism, during the Han and T'ang dynasties. It had only a clarifying and enriching influence on an already existing dance tradition which we know from early Confucian scriptures and the charming Wei and T'ang funeral figurines in terra-cotta. Indian dance, reflected in the form-language of Gupta art, was resuscitated in the Buddhist pantomimes under the later T'ang emperors. The Chinese tradition, in its turn, was broken through another national spectrum in Japan where Shintoism has preserved cult dances from prehistoric times. During the 2,600 years of Japanese history, there has been an unbroken continuity of dance development from the solemn, ceremonious symbolism of Bugaku, through Noh, to the modern Kabuki-Za of the seventeenth century. All these styles can be seen in living form in Japan today.

It is a joy to contemplate good Asiatic dances apart from the superficial attraction of gorgeous exotic costumes—glittering with brocades, gold, mirrorwork, jewelry, and enigmatic makeup—for the delight given by beautiful movements and poses. It is an absorbing study to learn these dances, the symbolism of their postures and gestures, the stories the symbols tell, the myths behind the stories, the world of experience and interpretation each offers. It is fascinating to see these various dance styles side by side, to observe the subtle differences of approach to the same themes, the varying ideals of beauty, life, the Divine. The dance, as the most delicate expression of human culture, is also the most revealing; a valuable indicium for the culture historian, an undiluted enjoyment for the art lover. It is to be feared that in this time of incisive political, social, and cultural revolutions, the exquisite traditions of Eastern dance are in danger of becoming blurred or sacrificed.

But this very crisis has a double aspect. Western ballet has reached the stage where it has become susceptible to the great traditions of Eastern dance. In the coming cultural synthesis in the time before us, the dance traditions of East and West may be united. Eastern dance has become known to the West. Indian, Javanese, Balinese, Thai, and Japanese dancers have celebrated triumphs in Europe and America. Eastern dance is attracting increasing interest from Western artists. Monographs have been written on Indian, Javanese, Balinese, Thai, Japanese, and Cambodian dances, but they are still insufficiently known, the synoptic approach is still lacking, the general books on the dance are still mute in the presence of its finest flowering in Asia.

This is the value of Xenia Zarina's art, her programs, which present these varying dance styles in all their authenticity, and this book in which she has set down her studies and observations. A former ballet star trained by Fokine, Mordkin, and Novikoff, she is, to my knowledge, the sole Western dancer conversant with Asiatic dance art as a whole. She has studied under the greatest teachers in Japan, Cambodia, Thailand, Java, Bali, and India, has lived in their very milieu for years, knows their stage, costumes, makeup, and attitude toward art. We cannot expect her to compete with these great masters, but she has absorbed their teachings as faithfully as a Western artist may ever be able to do, and she has an instinctive insight into the spiritual essence of each type. Moreover, she has had one experience none of these masters ever could acquire: the synoptic view of Asiatic dance as a multifoldly ramified, but fundamentally single, organic tradition. And she has tried to understand this unique experience, to formulate it in terms intelligible to the European and American dancer, art lover, and cultural historian. Eastern as well as Western connoisseurs have acclaimed and appreciated the art of Xenia Zarina. Her book, written with the unpretentiousness of the artist who honestly strives after an ideal of perfection, is a revelation of a world of the finest traditions of beauty. I wish it every possible success as a contribution toward the creation of a new humanism comprising East and West, based not only on the lore of the ancients, but on the best that mankind has ever brought forth.

HERMANN GOETZ, PH.D.
Heidelberg, Germany

Author's Preface

THE SOCIAL CHANGES occurring so rapidly in our present-day world often cause unsuspected repercussions, nowhere more than in the Orient. Traditions and customs, respected for centuries, are being overturned or cast aside. Kings, ruling princes, and maharajas are being dethroned or allowed only limited powers. Republics are being established in their stead.

In this process, cultural treasures, built up through the centuries, are being altered and, sometimes, destroyed and lost completely. As the arts must always reflect the spirit of their time, so it is that there is grave danger that the classical arts of certain Oriental countries may be buried—for a time at least—under a deluge of new but necessarily chaotic and unperfected expressions.

In the Orient, the great dance arts flourished in the serene atmosphere and protection of temples as an integral part of religious ritual and in the courts of rulers as an indispensable entertainment. Temples and rulers maintained with their ample funds groups of actor-dancers and musicians who were considered not as luxuries, but as essentials to life. So art grew in perfection and refinement through the ages. Now, with the establishment of new republics, headed by men of the people, struggling with economic difficulties, where will be found the leisure, culture, and funds to continue cultivation of the arts which were the very flower of those civilizations?

It was my privilege to study the classic dances of the Far East in the countries of their origin with the most celebrated teachers in each land, just before the world upheaval began, that is, from 1936 to 1947, when I watched the last British troops march, impeccable and dignified, out of India through the "Gateway to India," the great Victorian stone gateway of Bombay, to boats that took them to the outlying British warships, and home.

Then came pitiable waves of Indian refugees from Sind and Pakistan, where they and their ancestors had lived prosperously for centuries, leaving their homes and properties. Some lost their lives. Everyone who had a hotel room in Bombay was asked to share it with as many refugees as possible. A charming Indian girl named Pevi came to stay with me, and from her I learned many lessons in spiritual values, tolerance, patience, kindness, and gentleness.

In India the maharajas have been displaced or limited severely in their powers and finances. Thailand and Cambodia are threatened with drastic

xi

changes. Java is the seat of the Indonesian Republic. As for the Susuhunan of Surakarta and the Sultan of Djokjakarta, with their tranquil, languorous courts, those rulers who loved and protected the Javanese dance, what has become of them? Japan has recovered from terrible bombings, defeat, and occupation by the victors, but beloved Matsumoto Koshiro is dead.

This book is written in an attempt to record the traditions of the beautiful ancient dance techniques taught me by my illustrious teachers. I have sought to be faithful to their teachings and to the high artistic standards they impressed upon me.

The material given here is not an exhaustive study of the various dance styles. The field is too vast to give a complete study of even one dance style, not to mention six, in a single volume. The aim of this book is to set forth basic truths of the dance techniques, to point out the characteristics of each style that differentiate it from others, and to try to give some insight into the superb flowering of dance art in the six countries treated. In describing the Oriental dance techniques for Western dancers, I have compared them to ballet techniques, and used French ballet terms, since these are the international language of the dance. I offer this book with the sincere wish that it may be a help and guide to all who seek authentic information about Oriental dances.

I want to thank the renowned Orientalist Dr. Hermann Goetz for his understanding foreword. I am grateful to him and to his gentle wife for their encouraging friendship and gracious hospitality during my stay in Baroda, India. I thank Mr. and Mrs. Paul V. McNutt, the Kokusai Bunka Shinkokai, Mr. Senda, J. L. Moens, Michael Podoli, and all my many friends scattered around the world who helped me in so many ways and made this book possible.

XENIA ZARINA

Contents

Introduction

ALMOST THE FIRST thing the seeker after the dance becomes aware of in the Far East is the conception of and the attitude toward the dance as contrasted to the Occidental outlook. As all great religions have grown out of Asia, so too, the dance from India eastward begins with the gods. In each of the countries considered in this book, the dance is attributed to divine origin. Each land has its legend of the origin of the dance, and always it was the gods who created the dance and sent it to earth as a precious gift to gladden the hearts of mankind, to lift their spirits through contemplation of noble beauty, to inspire them with high ideals and ethics. This point is of utmost importance in understanding the dances of the Far East. We shall find altars and offerings in rehearsal rooms and in dressing rooms, reverential salutes to the teacher, and ceremonial salutes at the beginning and end of dance performances.

All the arts were employed to celebrate the gods, and rules for the preparation of an artist before beginning a work of art are given in those most venerable writings, the sacred *Vedas*. They are of immense interest to us here. They state: "The artist must first purify himself by bathing and fasting. He must then meditate in solitude and quiet upon the theme he is to represent until a clear picture of it appears in his mind." As in Vedic times, so today there can be no finer preparation for the creation of a work of art. Modern art critics may sigh and wish more artists followed the ancient rules.

While the Orient has looked toward spiritual values, the Occidental trend has been toward material and technical development, notably mechanical improvements. An Indian friend describes mechanics as "skill without sentiment." In general, one may say that the modern trend in Occidental dance technique is toward physical virtuosity, whereas Oriental dance technique is a vehicle for spiritual power. The dances of Eastern lands are usually dance dramas. They tell stories accompanied by chanted poetry or dramatic narratives. Classical Oriental dances have no breakneck stunts. Postures and poses are carefully studied from a sculptural viewpoint, and every gesture has a purpose. The ideal is to seek perfection of expressiveness rather than to astound the spectator by incredible feats. The Oriental dance may astonish by its beauty and perfection of movement by dramatic conception, or by sumptuousness of costume, but it does not aim to make the audience gasp; rather it seeks to give the audience a serene joy through contemplation of its message or to move it emotionally by revealing divine truths and eternal values.

Although East Asiatic dances stem principally from ancient Indian culture, in each country the dance today is distinct from that of India. There are two reasons for this. First, the imported Indian dance added its gifts to the native dance art. The natural taste of the indigenous peoples furthermore chose to retain certain elements of the Indian dance that pleased them, and to discard others that did not, the final blend evolving into a refined and characteristic form. Thus the dances of each land, Thailand, Cambodia, Java, and Bali, are truly expressive of the tastes and traditions of the people of these countries, although the impulse toward a great dance art came from India long ago. Second, the dance in India also has evolved over centuries. A comparative study of the dancing figures in Indian sculpture through the ages shows a great variety in posture, dance figures, costumes, and general feeling. Indian dance connoisseurs are in general accord that the classic dances of "Greater India" (Ceylon, Burma, Thailand, Cambodia, Java, and Bali) represent the preservation of the dances of ancient India, which are forgotten by modern India.

The world's oldest record of the art and technique of the dance is Indian. It is the fifth *Veda* (the *Natya Veda* or *Natya Sastra*), and it gives all the rules, postures, and gestures for human expression through the dance. These rules are still used in Indian dance, and indeed they apply to all classic dance art, for they are basic. Exactly when the *Veda*s were written is not known, but it was at least thirty centuries ago.

The fundamental principles of classical dance technique are identical whether in European ballet, or in Japanese, Thai, Cambodian, Javanese, Balinese, or Indian dance dramas. The torso position presents a straight spine and level shoulders; the positions of the feet accord with the five foot positions and the half-toe positions of European ballet. The fifth position is seldom used in Oriental dance, as very little aerial work comes into play, but Oriental dance adds some foot positions and foot movements not seen in European ballet; as samapada: feet close together, toes pointing front; ancita: the foot, vertical to the extended leg, rests on its heel, displaying the sole and toes; the Kathakali manner of placing the feet; the foot movements used both in the Japanese Noh-walk and in the Javanese kapang-kapang walk by which the dancers seem motivated by outside forces, not of their own wills, or as though they were suspended on strings like puppets. A dreamlike, uncanny impression is transmitted to the spectators by these remarkable modes of progression.

The manipulation of the arms in all Asiatic dances conforms to the laws of movement stated by François Delsarte, although the movements may seem curious and unusual to Western eyes. The knees are the springs of the human body, and their use in all types of dance is to give flow and pliancy to the movements. However, Oriental dancers flex the knees more deeply and more continuously than European dancers; and there are the costumes, which exercise great influence on body movements.

There are four misconceptions current which I would like to try to rectify to facilitate Western understanding of East Asiatic dances. The first is that a set technique crushes individuality and personality. In an ancient Sanskrit work, the *Abhinaya Darpana* of Nandikesvara, the Lord of Creation, Brahma, explains that the human actor attains to perfect art only through conscious discipline and not through impulse. All action must be carefully prescribed and studied. Nothing must be left to chance. The text of the play is the same, whoever the actor. The score of a musical composition remains the same, whoever the musician. So also the action, the dance, must be ordered. It is the action, not the actor, that is essential to the play. The secret of all art lies in self-forgetfulness. That is, the artist must submerge himself in the part he plays, in the message he is to transmit.

From these words of ancient wisdom it is clear that "self-expression," "asserting one's personality," is in defiance of artistic canons and can never be true and perfect art. Art is order and discipline, not chaos. But within the boundaries set by any art, the personality of the artist has ample scope. I witnessed several examples of the fact that technique does not crush personality when I watched different actors play the same role on successive nights. Those whose technique was closer to perfection had greater mastery over their role and therefore more freedom and more magnetism over the audience so that their personalities shone with greater luminosity.

The second misconception is that all Oriental dances are alike. One may as well say, all books are alike, just black type on white paper. To understand a book or a dance, one must not make superficial observations, but must read and study intelligently. The outstanding characteristics of the six types of dance discussed in this book show fundamental differences in the summary below.

Indian Bharat Natyam: Highly hieratic, symmetrical poses and choreography; vigorous rhythms; heavy downbeats.

Thai and Cambodian: Narrative dances; use of speaking gestures; asymmetrical poses and choreography; extreme flexation (back-turning) of fingers; curving lines; light; allegro rhythms; upward accent.

Javanese Court Dances—Serimpi and Bedoyo: Two-dimensional poses, symmetrical choreography; abstract; unworldly in sentiment; extremely slow; languorous, flowing rhythms.

Balinese Legong: Sharp-angled poses, abrupt transitions, intense, vibrant; striking eye movements and sideways jerking of the head (*engotan*); rapid rhythms with many changes of accent and tempo.

Japanese Nihon Buyo: Poetic themes of delicate sentiments, high comedy or tragic themes. Dramatic hands illustrating or suggesting the story of the accompanying song. Varied rhythms evolving harmoniously. Counterpoint.

The third misconception is that Oriental dancers are almost nude. The dance in all the farther Oriental lands is a ceremony with religious associations more or less apparent. As participants in such, the dancers are always garbed in the richest and most elaborate vestments, often identical to the ceremonial dress of royalty. Far from appearing nude, they are covered from neck to ankle in the most costly and beautiful articles of clothing, usually representing the ceremonial garments of ancient times. In the following chapters the costumes are listed and described in detail.

And now, the fourth misconception, the glamorous idea of temple dancers. When Thailand, Cambodia, and Java were Brahmanic, and the Sivaistic cult flourished, there were corps of temple dancers attached to the temples for the ritual dances that formed an important part of the cult ceremonies. But when Buddhism overcame Brahmanism, the ceremonies were simplified, and temple dances were excluded. When Java became Moslem, about 1535, there was still less chance for temple dancers since Islam looks with official disapproval on dancing, especially dances associated with former religious beliefs. Even court and entertainment dances, which had existed side by side with temple dances for the entertainment of the people and their rulers, had to go into hiding for a time. The great temples of Siva and Vishnu in Java, Thailand, and Cambodia have lain in deserted ruins for more than a thousand years. There are today no temple dancers in Buddhist Thailand, Buddhist Cambodia, or in Moslem Java, though in Cambodia, Madame Say Sang Van's troupe dances for tourists at Angkor on the terrace of a ruined temple. But these are not temple dancers, attached to the temple, supported by it, dedicated, consecrated and inaccessible, as the term originally implied.

In Bali, dance dramas are presented in the forecourt of the temple, under the sacred waringen tree, and in certain temple ceremonies old priests and priestesses dance rituals by torchlight. However, there are no dancers attached exclusively to Balinese temples, who live there, sacred and inviolate. A Balinese temple would be a little exposed to live in, being just a series of courts open to the sky, surrounded by sculptured walls with niches for offerings.

Nevertheless, there still do exist real temple dancers. You will find then in Japan at Shinto temples. They perform veritable cult dances of ancient origin, which are mentioned in the chapter on Japanese dance.

You will find temple dancers also in South India in Sivaistic temples where the cult is still practiced as in ancient days. These dancers are called deva dasis. They are dedicated to the service of the god by heritage, tradition, and actual practice. They celebrate the glory of the Divine by the most ancient system of dance known in India. It is called Bharat Natyam or Indian dance, for Natya means dance and Bharat is the ancient name of India. Bharata is also the name of the legendary author of the *Natya Sastra,* and furthermore, the three syllables bha, ra, and ta, signify the three fundamental elements of the dance: *bhava, raga,* and *tala,* that is, emotion, melody, and rhythm.

Classic
Dances
of the Orient

Classic Dances
of India

Origin of the Dance

THE EARLIEST RECORD of the dance that exists today comes to us from Vedic times. The Vedic writings are ancient and are supposedly of divine origin, being attributed to Brahma, Lord of Creation. When the four *Vedas* had been composed, Lord Brahma, seated in Yoga posture, composed from them the Fifth *Veda*, the *Natya Veda*. This was communicated by Brahma to the sage Bharata Muni who wrote it down as the *Natya Sastra*. In the *Natya Sastra*, the rules governing human movement for expressive purposes are given. Brahma explained the significance of dramatic art: "It is not to flatter any party but to represent the true and essential character of the world. The theatre and dance are to afford a means of entertainment in the world, and a place of audience for the Vedas, for philosophy, for history and other matters."

The sage, Bharata Muni, after receiving this communication from Brahma, and writing it as the *Natya Sastra*, formed a group of the Apsarases (heavenly dancers), the Gandharvas (heavenly musicians), and the Kinnaras (celestial singers), and gave a performance in the presence of Lord Siva. After witnessing this performance, Siva instructed his chief disciple Tandu to teach Bharata Muni the Tandava (masculine style of dance). Also, Siva's consort, Goddess Parvati, taught him the Lasya (feminine style of dance). Bharata Muni then taught the other sages, and thus the dance spread throughout the world.

1

Lord Siva is known as Nataraja, Lord of the Dance. His great cosmic dance is the symbol of the rhythmic creation of order out of chaos, for the ancient sages knew what science has lately discovered: that each and every thing has its own vibration and responds to the proper rhythm. Siva's dance established cosmic rhythm and harmony among all things. Siva's divine dance had 108 poses. These poses are sculptured on the great Sivaistic temple of Chidambaram in South India and form the basis of the Indian classic dance.

In the *Natya Sastra* it is written that the art of the dance brings fame, prosperity, happiness, and knowledge. It makes one liberal, generous, steady, and enlightened. It wards off misery, covetousness, and jealousy. This art gives the highest satisfaction and bliss. Were it not so, the gods and divine sages would not have been attracted to it.

The *Natya Sastra* divides the dance into three groups: Natya which is dance drama, or dances that tell a story; Nritya which is song and dance combined; and Nritta, which is pure rhythmic movement without any meaning except the expression of a mood or state of emotion. Also, there is Abhinaya, the art of speaking through gestures and postures timed to music. In the *Abhinaya Darpana* (Mirror of Gesture, translated into English by Ananda Coomaraswamy), it is stated: "wherever the hands go, there the eyes should follow. Wherever the eyes go, there the mind. Wherever the mind goes, there the feeling. Wherever the feeling goes, there the mood (*rasa*) or flavour is found." All this may be further clarified by the understanding that the terms *actor* and *dancer* are synonymous throughout India and the Far East.

Before beginning a performance, the troupe offers prayers with flowers to dedicate themselves and the play, to implore the blessing of the gods, and for the successful rendering of the guru-upadesha (the teaching) so that it may be an honor to their guru, or teacher.

Types of Dances

From its ancient beginning, the classic dance of India has gone through many phases and forms during the passing centuries. There were religious cult dances, court dances, wandering theatre troupes, and folk dances which were part of village life. All these still remain today. In different parts of India the dance took on different character and forms and costumes, corresponding to the taste and needs of the community. At different epochs these changed again. Sculptures and paintings on temples, palaces, and elsewhere show some of the evolution of the dance. Today, in India, four distinct types of classic dance exist.

Kathak is a North Indian style evolved during Mogol times.

Manipuri is performed in Assam, Eastern India; evolved from local folk dances.

Kathakali is conserved in Malabar, South India, a purely masculine style of dance with remarkable facial makeup and elaborate hand gestures, facial expressions, and technique.

Bharat Natyam is the most ancient and classic form of dance dating from Vedic times. It is a Sivaistic cult dance conserved in the temples of Siva in South India and performed by the Deva Dasis, essentially feminine in style. Mohini Attam in Kerala, South India, is a simplified form of Bharat Natyam.

The technique of Kathak is simpler than that of the elaborate Kathakali and Bharat Natyam. Hand gestures and ankle bells are used. The dances are Mogol court dances or tell Radha-Krishna stories. Kathak dances are in the class of entertainment dances; the element of religious fervor or devotion is not present in them. The Nautch dances belong to the Kathak class, and their costumes resemble those of Mogol paintings: very large skirt, sometimes transparent, worn over tight leg-fitting trousers, a tight-fitting jacket with long or short sleeves, and a veil covering the head and falling behind. Ankle bells and jewelry complete the costume for women. Male dancers wear tight-fitting trousers, and ample-skirted coat reaching to the knees, a Mogol turban, sash, and ankle bells. One of the most noted teachers of Kathak was Menaka (Lady Sokhey) who died in the summer of 1947. Menaka was known and loved in Europe where she had been a pioneer in presenting authentic Indian dances. She was so absorbed in the dance that all her efforts, time, and money were spent on her school near Bombay.

The Manipuri dances are delightful to all audiences. They tell the popular Radha-Krishna and Gopi stories in an attractive, uncomplicated technique infused with an atmosphere of devotion and amorous sentiment. The stories tell of the love of the Gopis (girls who herded cows) and Radha for the pastoral god, Krishna. The costume worn by the Gopis is charming: a bell-shaped skirt with a deep border of embroidery and mirrors; a short-sleeved jacket leaving the waist bare; the hair piled in a high cone on the center of the head or off-center at one side, covered by a transparent veil which hangs down the back and falls over the shoulders; a sash and jewelry completing the costume.

The technique of Kathakali is a tremendous study, strenuous and elaborate. Kathakali is a purely masculine type of dance, and to become proficient the actors have to undergo a six- to ten-year period of training under a recognized guru. My own teacher, Kumar Jayakar, told me of a remarkable preparation for a Kathakali dancer which he himself underwent. This is a "massage" by the feet of a man specialized in the art. The would-be Kathakali dancer lies prostrate while the "masseur" hangs by his hands from the limb of a tree or overhead *barre*, and with his feet "massages"—pommels and bruises—the body of the poor victim who wails in agony. Often this first treatment completely discourages the would-be dancer, but if he persists, after three or four treatments it is no longer painful but becomes, in fact, exceptionally stimulating. Kathakali plays are written in mixed verse and prose. The actors' dialogues are sung in Malayalam although the plays are written in Sanskrit and Malayalam. The hand gesture repertoire is vast and complicated, the facial gestures are often violent and terrifying to the spectators, and the foot rhythms are intricate and powerful. Often the earth trembles beneath the feet of an actor. Kathakali facial makeup is unique. The actor's face is covered with a paste made of rice flour and lime called *chuti,* and his features are built up until he is unrecognizable. The paste mask is then painted according to the role the actor is to play: king, demon, god, demigod, brahmin, sage, ambassador, wandering minstrel, and others. The masks are colored red, green, pink, yellow, white, and blue, and beards are also colored indicatively. The feminine roles do not require such exaggerated makeup and painting. The actors wear great hoopskirts and imposing headdresses glittering with mirrors and trembling with ornaments. When the time comes for an actor's entrance, attendants hold a curtain about five feet long and four feet wide, with emblems of a lotus or a sign of Siva or Vishnu upon it, before the actor's face. At the proper moment, they lower the curtain, and the actor appears, standing in a deep *plié.* In a theatre, the Kathakali actor may enter from the wings or in the traditional way just described. Kathakali is perhaps the most vigorous and virile dancing I have ever seen. The sharp, elastic movements of the body, the energetic arm movements, the complicated hand gestures, the powerful foot rhythms and extravagant facial expressions, all accompanied by and accentuated by thundering drums, resounding gongs, and metallic effects, build up an intense atmosphere and excitement that never fail to move the spectator. This is the Tandava type of dance par excellence. The great teacher and exponent of Kathakali, Guru Sankaran Nambudripad—first discovered by the poet Vallathol, then brought out and presented by Uday Shankar—is now dead. His great talent and presence are mourned. Now the most famous dancer and teacher of Kathakali is Gopinath, who lives and works in Madras.

Bharat Natyam has nine parts or movements, and the complete dance requires two and a half to three hours to perform. The different parts may be presented separately as solos or group dances. The nine parts of Bharat Natyam are described under Dance Performances.

Musical accompaniment is supplied by a drum, violin or other string instrument, backing up a singer. The head, eyes, eyebrows, eyelids, eyeballs, lips, and neck are very important to the interpretation of the songs, for the spectators' attention is centered there. The appropriate movements are taught by the guru and are recorded in the Sanskrit texts on dance and drama. The form of Bharat Natyam today is somewhat changed from the time of the *Natya Sastra*. Its present choreography was the work of four Nattuvans of the Tanjore court. They were brothers who were especially endowed artistically and who resuscitated the languishing dance and music of their time. One of them was the first to introduce the violin into Carnatic music. They were contemporary with the Travancore king Swathi Thirunal. The greatest living dancers of Bharat Natyam today are Balasaraswati, Rukmini Devi, Srimati Shanta Rao, and Mrinalini Sarabhai. Balasaraswati and Rukmini Devi live in Madras where the latter has a school known as Kalakshetra.

Training for the Dance

In ancient times, and until India became independent, a number of Indian states kept dancers and musicians permanently attached to the court for the entertainment of the ruler, his family, and guests. These artists also taught the royal children, and thus continued the cultivation and love of Indian arts. When I was visiting Baroda State, I had the pleasure of hearing the court musicians and seeing the court dancers at a private showing arranged for me by Mr. Doctor, Director of the Maharaja's Conservatory of Music. The music of the orchestra was the sweetest Indian music I had ever heard, and the dances were Bharat Natyam. His Late Highness, the Gaekwar Sayaji Rao of Baroda, kept at his court Gaurabai, one of the finest Bharat Natyam dancers of that time. Gaurabai was the Baroda Court Dancer for over fifty years. The present Maharaja of Baroda and his father kept at court a group of musicians and two girl dancers from Tanjore, South India. The leader of this group was Chandrasen

Pillai, a star pupil of the greatest of all Bharat Natyam gurus, the venerable Pandanullar Meenakshisundaram Pillai of Tanjore. I was so enraptured by the dancing of these two Deva Dasis that Mr. Doctor arranged for me to study with Chandrasen Pillai. This was a very special opportunity for me to learn from a real Nattuvan.

Every afternoon Chandrasen Pillai came faithfully and punctually to teach me for two solid hours the pure, hieratic movements of the dance of the Deva Dasis. After I had learned the movements, he would sing or count the tempos as I danced. His language is South Indian, or Telugu. As I did not know any Telugu and only a few words of Hindustani, and he, only a few of English, our communication depended mainly on pantomime, which was rather fun and certainly challenged our ingenuity. With Chandrasen Pillai I learned the beautiful Alarippu, Varnam, and Tillana parts of Bharat Natyam.

When I was to return to Bombay, Chandrasen Pillai gave me the name of a friend with whom I could continue my studies. This friend was Kumar Jayakar, a young master of Bharat Natyam who speaks excellent English and knows how to explain the interesting backgrounds, purpose, and meanings of the dance movements. He is an intensely sincere young man, and his love of the dance is evidenced by the fact that he went to the south to study with the great guru, Pandanullar Meenakshisundaram Pillai, but not being able to afford three hundred rupees (about $100) a lesson, he entered the service of the guru as personal servant to be near him, and to learn. Kumar Jayakar has a fund of valuable information, and is preparing a book on Indian dance with diagrams and music notations. My lessons with Jayakar were invaluable in perfecting what I had already learned with Chandrasen Pillai, and in extending my understanding of Indian dance.

Costume for the Dance

The traditional Tanjore costume worn today consists of ankle-length narrow trousers made of brocade over which is draped a 9-yard sari. The pleats of the sari hanging in front are taken between the legs and tucked into the belt behind, giving a trouser effect when seen from the back, and a skirt effect from the front. This style of dress gives freedom of leg action. A sash of beautiful material is tied about the waist and hangs in front. A short choli or jacket with short sleeves, made of rich material, a little cap, earrings, nose ring, bracelets, hair ornaments, ankle bells, and gold belt complete the costume. The hair is worn in a long plait down the back and ornamented with flowers. Dancers carved on ancient temples, who supposedly were "temple dancers," dressed very differently: they wore light, transparent costumes that revealed all the alluring beauty of line and movement of their bodies. Costumes and customs change with changing times. "In the past even queens became dancing girls and dancing girls became saints," wrote an Indian author.

Masks and Makeup

No masks whatever are used in Bharat Natyam, Kathak, Manipuri, or Kathakali, the four classic schools of Indian dance. The nearest suggestion of a mask is the extraordinary facial makeup of the Kathakali dancers, as described above.

Facial makeup aims to make the dancer's face as attractive as possible and to bring out the features for expressive purposes. The eyes are outlined in black; the eyebrows are defined and arched, sometimes outlined above by tiny white dots. The inevitable caste mark, the red dot on the forehead between the brows, is sometimes replaced for the theatre by an ornamental dot that glitters in the stage lights.

The palms of the hands are painted red. This enhances the effect of the mudras.

A red line is painted around the foot just above the sole and at the edge of the sole. The toes are painted red, and one band of red is drawn across from the ball of the foot to the base of the little toe.

Dance Properties

No dance properties are used. The whole art lies in the use of the hands and eyes. Mimicry, when used, is so perfect that a spectator would vow he had seen a ball, a jug, or other property.

Music for the Dance

The instrumentation is very simple, comprising a drum, a violin or other stringed instrument, a flute or other woodwind, and a singer who chants in Telugu, the South Indian language. As in the dance exercises, rhythms are in slow, medium, and fast tempos, falling suddenly again into slow tempo, which gives contrast and excitement to the performance.

Dance Performances

While Bharat Natyam is of ancient origin and a true ritual temple dance, it is now studied all over India in almost every dance school. During the Victorian era, dancing was looked down upon, frowned upon; whereas now, the ability to dance Bharat Natyam is a definite social asset. Indian girls—and boys, too, despite the fact that Bharat Natyam is a traditionally feminine type of dance—study it devotedly. Every serious dance program includes Bharat Natyam. Sometimes a girl and a boy do a Bharat Natyam dance together as a duet, a modern innovation, but a pleasing one. Such programs are of course given in theatres or in spacious private homes, but not in temples. The ancient method of lighting for the dances was to place a row of candles or small oil lamps before the dancers like footlights. I was invited to such a performance in a wealthy home. The effect of the flickering soft lights was delightful. Such effects are sometimes used in theatres instead of electric spotlights and footlights.

The traditional Bharat Natyam performance, entirely dedicated to this style of dance, has nine parts, and is a solo performance by a highly trained woman dancer.

Alarippu is always the opening dance, a dance of greeting and invocation. It is composed of lovely hieratic postures and slow rhythms that increase suddenly to complicated coordination of footbeats and hand movements in fast tempos.

Jatisvaram is the following dance with five involved rhythms of 3, 4, 5, 7, and 9 beats to the measure.

Sabdam, the third, is a song in Telugu to Lord Krishna. The singer's words are interpreted by the dancer through hand gestures and facial expressions. This gives the dancer a rest between Jatisvaram and the following dance; although between verses of Sabdam, the dancer executes various adaus (short, complicated dance sequences).

Svarajati follows. This is one of the most elaborate of the dance sequences, with lovely dance movements.

Varnam, which comes next, is a long dance to a song in Telugu praising Lord Krishna. Each verse is sung several times, accompanied by dance sequences in slow, medium, and fast tempos.

Javali is an erotic poem sung by the singer and interpreted by the dancer with hand gestures, eyes, and interpolated adaus.

Padam is a song about Parvati's love for Lord Siva, sung by the singer and
acted by the dancer, who also executes several adaus.

Tillana, the culminating dance, is a strenuous and complicated one. Most
of the adaus are in fast tempo. The sculptural lines of the dance postures,
after rapid turns and dips, are as exciting to watch as they are hard to do.

Sloka, sung in Sanskrit and interpreted by the dancer's hand gestures, concludes the Bharat Natyam performance which lasts from two and a half
to three hours. The audience, however, never tires of watching, fascinated, the beautiful movements, the impelling rhythms, and continual
variety in the traditional sequence of Bharat Natyam.

In any discussion of Indian dances, the marvelous dances of Kandy
must not be omitted. Many people had told me, "Oh, don't fail to see
the wonderful dances of Kandy"—but what they were like, who the
dancers were, how costumed, how they danced—not a word, only that they
were "wonderful." I was totally unprepared when, attending an important
program of all-Indian dances in a Bombay theatre, before my amazed eyes
a superb creature in starched white skirt, bare from the waist up, torso and
arms covered with handsome silver jewelry, and a glittering silver headdress, appeared on the stage. He leaped into his dance, shaking, quivering,
with great bounds ending in deep *pliés* between the vibrating postures.
His arms writhed continually, with meaningful hand gestures; his eyes
shot glances now here, now there; fingers trembled; feet pounded out the
complicated rhythms without pause; all the movements were accentuated
and adorned by ankle bells and the swinging, sparkling silver jewelry:
the wide handsome black, red, and silver belt with a long swinging pendant
in front; the dog-collar necklace, elaborate pectoral, armlets, bracelets,
great silver ear ornaments, and that stunning silver headdress that enhanced every head movement with its own scintillating, flashing oscillations.
And this thrilling display went on and on and on until I wondered how
any human body could have such tremendous energy and endurance.
Thus must Lord Siva have danced when he created the Tandava type of
dance to display masculine virility. Thus must Siva have danced when, at
the beginning of time, he created all things by his divine and infinitely
varied rhythms.

Deva Dasis: Social Organization

Bharat Natyam is part of temple life, and although with royal pat-
ronage it also became a courtly art, it still retains its status as a sacred

ritual or cult dance. It is danced by Deva Dasis and taught by Nattuvans, hereditary musicians who are often the sons of Deva Dasis. Nattuvans and Deva Dasis are a hereditary caste of musicians and dancers. They have their own caste laws, quite distinct from other castes, which regulate inheritance, marriage, rules of etiquette, and social customs. Their own councils see that these caste laws are followed.

Long ago in India a matriarchal system prevailed all over the country, but today it persists only in South India. The Deva Dasi caste is matriarchal. Sons and daughters inherit equally, contrary to Hindu custom, and the line of descent is from the mother's side. Those daughters who are too plain to become attractive Deva Dasis marry men of their caste. The others are carefully taught dancing, singing, the art of dressing well, and *ars amoris*. The sons usually become musicians, and earn their living by playing music, teaching singing and dancing to girls, and music to boys. These men are called Nattuvans.

Dancing girls are dedicated to a temple before puberty, usually between the ages of six and eight. A girl may dedicate herself to temple service in several ways. Old Hindu documents list the dancing girls as follows:

Datta: one who gives herself as a gift to the temple.

Bikrita: one who sells herself to a temple.

Bhritya: one who offers herself as a temple servant for the prosperity of her family.

Bhakta: one who joins a temple out of devotion.

Hrita: one who is enticed away and presented to a temple.

Alankara: one who, being well trained in her profession and richly adorned, is presented to a temple by a king or noble.

All applications to join a temple must be made through the senior dancing girl to the temple authorities, who then investigate the applicant's record. If she is accepted, some rice and money are given to her family to defray the cost of the ceremony. On the chosen day, the girl goes to the temple, bathed and cleanly dressed, bringing two new cloths, betel, and other offerings which she gives to the temple priest. The girl sits in the inner sanctuary, facing the deity. The priest kindles the fire and performs the traditional "marriage" ceremony, the girl being formally married to the god, to a sword, or to some other symbol of the deity. The marriage badge, *tali,* is tied around her neck; the priest teaches her the Panchakshara hymn if the temple is Sivaistic, or the Ashtakshara hymn if it is a temple to Vishnu. The Nattuvan then instructs her for the first time in the dance, a quantity of rice is given her by the temple authorities and she is taken home where the marriage festivities are celebrated for several days.

A dancing girl's duties are, as in olden times to carry the sacred light; to fan the idol; to sing and dance before the god. There are three types of Deva Dasis according to their duties:

Rajadasis: those who dance before the flagstaffs in the temples.

Devadasis: those who dance in temples dedicated to Siva.

Swadasis: those who dance only on special occasions.

All the sages who have written on the dance and song have stated the qualities a dancing girl should possess. Bharata Muni, the oldest and most interesting writer, says: "The dancing girl should be intelligent, should have a pure and chaste life; possess physical beauty; a sense of correct movements in pursuance of musical beats; emotional and intellectual fervor and a youthful surprise; know the whole of dramatic art and its correct display." In recent times, the Reverend M. Phillips wrote: "The dancing girls are highly accomplished women. They read, write, sing and play as well as dance. Hence, one of the great objections against the education of girls was 'We don't want our daughters to become dancing girls.' " Abbé Dubois wrote: "Of all the women in India, it is especially the courtesans who are most decently clothed."

A tragic fate to befall a woman in India is to become a widow, but a Deva Dasi, being married to a god, can never be widowed, so her presence is considered auspicious, and she is often invited to be present at marriages, to touch or prepare articles to be worn by the bride, and to walk at the head of wedding processions. Some Deva Dasis have amassed enormous fortunes and have given liberally to charity or to the erection of bridges, reservoirs, and other public works. In the past Deva Dasis enjoyed a considerable social position.

As soon as the new dancing girl is admitted to the temple, her training in dancing and singing begins. Much care is taken to keep her in perfect physical condition. Muscular exercises and the entire training are given under a guru according to the Vedic traditions. When the girl is sufficiently trained to appear before the public, a dedication ceremony is arranged in the temple where, before the deity, her guru, and a few invited guests, she sings and dances after performing the initial ritual of worship. This is the beginning of her career as a Deva Dasi. The girl's lessons continue with her Nattuvan during her temple life, and she shows her gratitude to her teacher by giving him some of her earnings as a Deva Dasi.

When a Dasi becomes too old or too ill to carry on her duties, she

applies to the temple authorities for permission to "remove her ear ornaments," that is, to resign. A ceremony is then performed at the maharaja's
palace at which she removes her ear-jewels. Her temple wages from then on
are slightly reduced because of her incapacity. When a Dasi dies, her funeral
pyre is lit by sacred fire brought from the temple.

With modern ideas and social reforms, some modifications and restric-
tions have been put upon the ancient Deva Dasi system. The Mysore State
government in 1910 prohibited the dedication of girls in state-controlled
temples. In 1930 the Madras government passed a resolution to en-
franchise Deva Dasis who hold land by virtue of their temple service, and
another bill was brought to prohibit the dedication ceremony in any
Hindu temple and to enable dedicated women to contract legal marriages.
Sawantawadi State, in 1930, raised the minimum age of dedication to
eighteen years, the Maharani of Travancore abolished the dedication of
girls in the temples maintained by her state, and, in 1944, Pudukottai
State abolished the Deva Dasi system in all state temples.

There are many interesting facets to the social system of the Dasis:
their moral values, their caste system, their folkways, and so on, but what
is most important to the world is that the Deva Dasis and their Nattuvans
are responsible for preserving in living, active form, from Vedic times to
the present, the wonderful system of dance known as Bharat Natyam,
recorded in the *Natya Sastra*. Until recent days the Deva Dasis and the
Nattuvans, as well as the Brahmins, have been almost the sole repositories
for the ancient and beautiful tradition of Indian dance and music. Indian
independence has since "cast its shadow before" in the form of keen and
widespead interest in and study of Indian arts.

Dance Technique

Note: The four schools of Indian dance have variations of the Bharat
Natyam school mudras, but even within this school, different teachers will
give some slight variations. Those given here appear to be the most standard.

POSITION OF THE HAND IN RELATION TO THE BODY

Abhimukha: palm opposite the face.
Adhomukha: palm facing downward.
Paranmukha: palm facing audience.
Tiryanmukha: hand at a slant.
Uttana: palm facing upward.

ABHIMUKHA

ADHOMUKHA

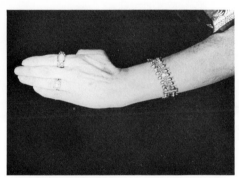

PARANMUKHA

(photos by Hans Stallforth)

TIRYANMUKHA

UTTANA

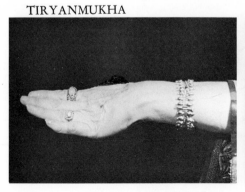

Foot Positions

Agratala: one-half toe position.
Ancita: heel resting on the ground, sole and toes raised.
Kuncita: similar to a ballet fifth position.
Nisanoru: similar to a ballet *plié*, but knees more deeply flexed.
Samapada: feet together, toes pointing forward.
Tryasra: similar to a ballet first position.

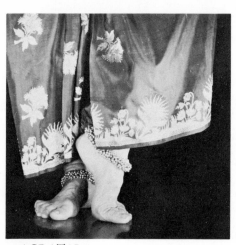

AGRATALA

AGRATALA (with both feet)

AGRATALA (behind), similar to ballet 4th position

ANCITA   KUNCITA

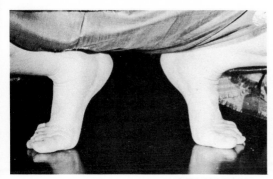
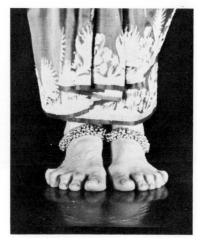

NISANORU

SAMAPADA

TRYASRA

ANKLE BELLS FOR INDIAN DANCES

Ankle bells are essential to all forms of Indian dance, not only to Bharat Natyam. They are worn in two strings of 30 to 52 or even more brass bells each. One string always has a higher tone, and this is tied on the left ankle. The lower-toned string is worn on the right ankle. The tassel, with which each string ends, lies on the instep. They must be tied carefully so as not to loosen and fall off during the dance. Their role is an important one, for their sound adds to the music and underlines each foot movement.

Bharat Natyam lessons begin with the Guru Vandanam, salutation to the teacher at the beginning and at the end of each lesson; also to the audiences at the beginning and at the end of each dance.

Stand with feet in samapada position; hands in sikaramudra, thumbs on shoulders, elbows open at sides.

Nisanoru (*plié*), opening feet to tryasra position, and opening arms in a large circle to the ground; hands in pataka mudra, fingertips touching ground. Look down at hands.

Rise to standing posture, feet in samapada position, and bring arms up in large circle to touch temples with fingertips in pataka mudra, palms facing out.

Join palms of hands before breast in Anjali, and bow. Repeat three times.

1. PATAKA (flag): a benediction, speaking, teaching, giving the law, prohibiting.

2. TRIPATAKA: a crown, a tree, the Vajra, symbol of Indra

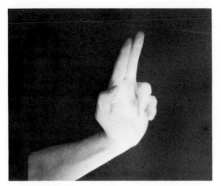

3. ARDHAPATAKA (one-half pataka): meaning "both."

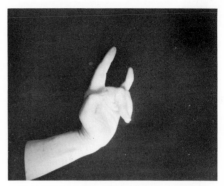

4. KARTARI-MUKHA (arrow shaft): separation, death, drawing an arrow.

5. MAYURA (peacock): renown, a peacock.

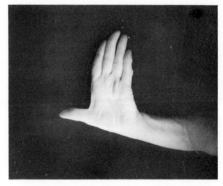

6. ARDHA-CHANDRA: half-moon.

7. ARALA: drinking nectar or drinking poison or sipping water.

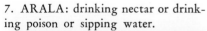

8. SUKATUNDA: shooting an arrow, revealing mystic things.

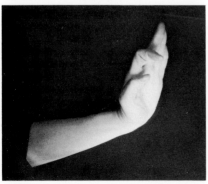

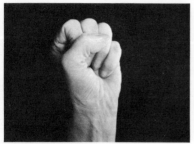

9. MUSTI (fist): fighting, war, strength, firmness, domination.

10. SIKHARA: symbol of Siva, love.

11. KAPITHA: symbol of the goddesses Lakshmi and Sarasvati, holding a flower. Represents a parrot, the symbol of the goddesses of learning.

12. KATAKA-MUKHA (opening in a link), picking flowers, holding a pearl or garland of flowers, applying perfume.

13. SUCI (needle): signifies "one," a demonstration, the sun, "listen!"

14. CHANDRA-KALA: signifies the crescent moon.

15. PADMAKOSA (lotus bud): means a fruit, a ball of flowers, a bud, anything round.

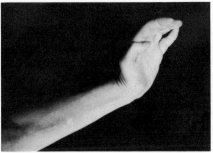

16. SARPA-SIRSA (cobra head): signifies a cobra, also a symbol of Siva-Omniscient.

17. MRGA-SIRSA (deer head): drawing three lines of paint or perfume or sandalwood paste on the brow.

18. SIMHA-MUKHA (lion face): represents a bull, a cow, deer.

19. ALAPADMA (full-blown lotus): signifies full-blown lotus, an offering of flowers.

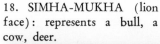

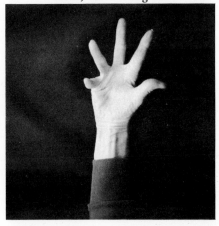

20. CATURA: means musk, gold, copper, oath, caste, sweetness, playful conversation.

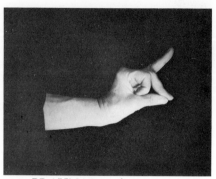

21. BRAHMARA (bee): represents a bee.

22. HAMSASYA (swan face): tying the marriage thread, instruction, pearls, painting, drawing lines, carrying garlands.

23. HAMSAVAKTRA: signifies instructing in wisdom, speaking, reading, meditation, singing, sound of a flute.

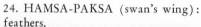

24. HAMSA-PAKSA (swan's wing): feathers.

25. MUKULA (bud): means a flower bud, eating, the God of Love.

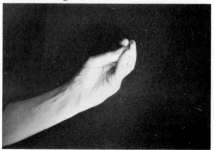

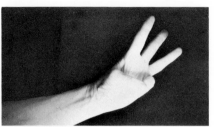

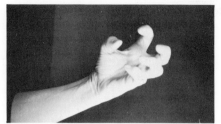

26. TRISULA (trident):
means three.

27. URNA-NABHA (spider):
means a claw, a tiger's jaws
(when two hands are combined).

28. BANA: indicating,
pointing out.

29. ANJALI (salutation): The hands
are held at the forehead for deities, before the face for important persons, before the breast for equals. Two Pataka
hands are joined palm to palm.

30. KAPOTA (dove): used for
taking oath, conversation with
elders, humility, acquiescence, receiving things. The hands are joined
at base, side, and fingertips.

31. KARTAKA (crab): means a
group, blowing the conch shell. The
fingers of the hands are interlocked.

32. SVASTIKA (crossed): with a gathering-in movement, means love, an embrace, peace. Two Pataka hands are crossed.

33. PUSPAPUTA (flower basket): offering of lights, offering of water, receiving gifts, offering gifts. Two Sarpasirsa hands, joined at sides.

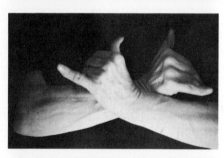

34. UTSANGA (embrace): means an embrace, modesty. Two Mrga-sirsa hands crossed on breast.

35. SIVA-LINGA: symbol of Siva. Left hand in Ardha-chandra. Right hand in sikara on top.

36. KATAKA-VARDHANA (link of increase): represents coronation, ritual, marriage blessing. Two Kataka hands crossed at wrists.

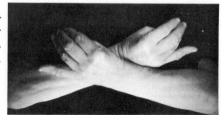

37. KARTARI-SVASTIKA: usage: trees, boughs of trees. Two Kartari hands crossed at the wrists. (*Photo by Hans Stallforth*)

38. SAKATA (car): means gestures of Raksasas (demons). Two Brahmara hands joined at thumbs and middle finger.

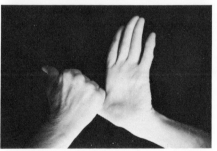

39. SANKHA (conch): usage, blowing the conch shell. Left hand in Ardha-chandra. Right hand in Sikara, grasping the Ardha-chandra (left) thumb.

40. CHAKRA (a wheel): with rotating movement, it means a wheel. Two Ardha-chandra hands, palm to palm.

42. PASA (noose): usage for enmity, noose. Two hands, back to back, forefingers crossed.

41. SAMPUTA (casket): means a casket or concealing things.

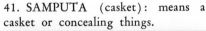

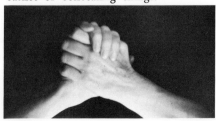

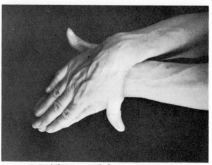

43. KILAKA (bond): used for affection, conversation of lovers. Two Mrga-sirsa hands linked by little fingers.

44. MATSYA (fish): represents a fish. Two Ardha-chandra hands, one atop the other.

45. KURMA (tortoise): represents a tortoise.

46. VARAHA (boar): represents a boar.

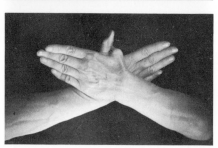

47. GARUDA (mythical eagle): used to refer to Garuda, the protector of mankind; also suggests any bird. Two Ardha-chandra hands with thumbs interlocked.

48. NAGA-BANDA (serpent tie): a pair of snakes (cobras). Two Sarpa-sirsa hands crossed at the wrists.

49. KHATVA (bed): used to suggest a bed. Two Kartari-mukha hands are joined at fingertips.

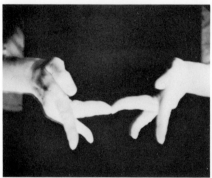

50. BHERUNDA (pair of birds): used to suggest pair of birds. Two Kapittha hands are crossed at wrists.

51. AVAHITTHA: Two Alapadma hands joined at wrists: means offering of flowers or the full-blown Lotus, symbol of Beauty and Purity.

52. KRISHNAVENU (flute of Krishna): symbol of and suggesting the pastoral god, Krishna. Two Mrga-sirsa hands joined by right thumb to left little finger.

Dance Exercises

After the Guru Vandanam exercises for footwork are practiced, stand in tryasra (first position) *plié;* hands placed palms out on lower part of back at hip height, fingers pointing diagonally down; torso straight; head level; eyes looking forward. In this position for an hour or so, various foot-beats are practiced with accented downbeats so that the ankle bells ring properly. Sometimes the row of dancers moves to the right, or to the left, or in a circle, or simply on place. Each exercise is practiced in three tempos: slow, medium, and fast (adagio, moderato, and presto). During all this time the knees have remained in a deep *plié,* very tiring and painful to the thigh muscles of a novice. After these exercises are learned (they are repeated at the beginning of each lesson), the various hand positions are learned. Then there are short sequences of foot-beats combined with hand positions (adaus), to be learned. The exercises and adaus are accompanied by rhythmic counts (bols) which are chanted by the guru and the pupils together during lessons. The adaus are afterward combined to form the finished dance. An adau compares to an *enchaînement* in ballet, that is, a sequence of dance steps.

Exercise I: Bols (count aloud): "teya-te, teya-te." On "teya," raise right foot, on "te," stamp right foot. Repeat with left foot.
Stamp right foot, stamp left foot in slow even tempo 8 times. Repeat in moderate tempo 8 times, then in fast tempo 8 times.

Exercise II: Bols: "teya-te, teya-te."
Stamp right foot twice, stamp left foot twice. Repeat 8 times in each tempo: slow, medium, fast.

Exercise III: Bols: "teyun-datta, te-ya-a."
Stamp right foot twice slowly, bols, "teyun-datta"; three times fast, bols, "te-ya-a"; repeat with left foot. Repeat 8 times in each tempo, keeping deep flexation of the knees: slow, medium, fast.

Exercise IV: Bols: "teyun-datta, te-ya."
Right leg extends to right side, foot in ancita position. Bols: "teyun."
Right foot returns to tryasra (first position). Bols, "datta."
Left leg extends to left side, foot in ancita position. Bols, "te."
Left foot returns to tryasra. Bols, "ya."
Repeat 8 times in each tempo: slow, medium, fast.

Exercise V: Bols: "teyun-datta, te-ya. Teyun-datta, te-ya."
Repeat the movements of each leg as in Exercise IV, twice to each side.
Right leg extends to right side, foot in ancita position. Bols, "teyun."
Stamp foot in tryasra. Bols, "datta." Right leg extends to right side,
foot in ancita position. Bols, "te." Stamp foot in tryasra. Bols, "ya."
Repeat with left leg. Repeat 8 times in each tempo: slow, medium, fast.

Exercise VI: Bols: "teyun-datta, te-ya; teyun-datta, te-ya."
On "teyun," extend right leg to right side, foot in ancita position. On
"datta," return right foot to tryasra and stamp. On "te," extend left leg
to left side, foot in ancita position.
On "ya," return left foot to tryasra with stamp.
On "teyun," place right foot behind left in kuncita (fifth position).
On "datta," stamp left foot in place.
On "te," extend right leg to right side, foot in ancita.
On "ya," return right foot to tryasra with stamp.
Repeat 8 times in each tempo: slow, medium, fast.

Exercise VII: Bols: "te-ya-ta," moving in a circle.
On "te," stamp with right foot in second position.
On "ya," stamp with left foot in agratala one-half-toe, close to right foot.
On "ta," lower left heel to floor.
When one circle has been completed, reverse the circle so that the left
foot leads; the legs always in *plié* position.
Repeat 8 times in each tempo: slow, medium, fast.

Exercise VIII: Bols: "teya-datta," moving in circle.
On "te," stamp with right foot in agratala in second position.
On "ya," lower the right heel to the floor.
On "da," stamp with left foot in agratala in second position.
On "ta," lower left heel to the floor.
Continue thus in a circle, always in second position, *plié*.
When one circle has been completed, reverse the circle so that the left
foot leads. Repeat 8 times in each tempo: slow, medium, fast.

Exercise IX: Bols: "te-ya-ta," moving in a line to right side.
On "te," hop onto both half-toes.
On "ya," stamp with right foot in a small second position.
On "ta," bring left foot close to right with stamp.
Continue 8 times in each tempo: slow, medium, fast. Reverse to left.

Exercise X: Bols: "te-ya-datta" in place.

On "te," stamp right foot in tryasra.

On "ya," extend right foot straight front, foot in ancita.

On "dat," stamp with left foot in place.

On "ta," stamp right foot beside left in tryasra.

Repeat with left foot.

Repeat 8 times in each tempo: slow, medium, fast.

Exercise XI: Bols: "teya-datta-te-ya-ta" in place.

On "teya," stamp right foot in tryasra.

On "datta," stamp left foot in tryasra.

On "teya," extend right leg forward, foot in ancita, and step on left foot as it remains in tryasra.

On "ta," stamp right foot in tryasra beside left.

Repeat on left side.

Repeat 8 times in each tempo: slow, medium, fast.

Exercise XII: Bols: "te-ya-teya-da-ta."

On "te," stamp right foot in tryasra.

On "te," stamp left foot in tryasra.

On "te," stamp right foot in tryasra.

On "teya," extend right leg forward, foot in ancita, and step on left foot in place.

On "ta," stamp right foot in tryasra beside left.

Repeat, starting with left foot. Continue 8 times in each tempo: slow, medium, fast.

Exercise XIII: Bols: "te-ya-teya-da-ta."

On "te," hop on both one-half-toes.

On "ya," step on left foot.

On "teya," extend right foot front in ancita and step back on left foot.

On "da," bring right foot back to tryasra with a stamp.

On "ta," stamp left foot in tryasra.

Repeat, but reversing feet. Continue 8 times in each tempo: slow, medium, fast.

Points to observe in the execution of exercises and dances:

When the dancer hops onto half-toes, the shoulders should not rise, but should maintain their level. This is accomplished by knee action.

A happy expression should be maintained.

Each step must be firmly placed, like a stamp.

The torso must be kept in saustavanaga (perfect symmetry).

Bharat Natyam must be executed with softness, grace, and flexibility.

Note: The above exercises are only for feet and legs, to give the strength and firmness required for Indian dances. These and the mudras are the first preparation for a dancer. After these are mastered, arm movements with appropriate mudras are combined with foot movements in sequences called "adaus." Adaus are comparable to ballet *enchaînements,* or dance sequences. Finally, adaus are combined into a dance—Alarippu, Jetisvaram, or any one of the nine parts of Bharat Natyam.

Concluding Thoughts

Foreshadowing the freedom of India and the Indian renaissance was the active interest of the whole country in a revival of their own arts. Now that India is independent, dancing, painting, and music are being studied eagerly all over the country. Pupils come from far to study with a celebrated master, although the expense is considerable. Art exhibits and dance performances are frequent and packed by attentive, enthusiastic audiences. The Indian National Theatre has been established, and sponsors dance groups that tour India. Painters use dancers and dance themes more often than any other subject. Dance schools flourish, and children are studying dance as part of their education. All these signs are full of promise.

With independence causing reduced budgets and other necessary shifting of traditional practices, ways are being sought to preserve the venerable and glorious tradition of Indian court and temple dances, for it is a great art, eternal in its appeal. It has been said that three things immortalize a nation: religion, wisdom, and art. India has all three.

Chandrasen Pillai.

Kumar Jayakar.

Chandrasen Pillai demonstrating
a position from Bharat Natyam.

Kumar Jayakar demonstrat-
ing mudras: right hand,
brahmara mudra (a bee);
left hand, alapadma mudra
(a full-blown flower).

Bharat Natyam danced by two Deva Dasis, court dancers to H.H. the Maharaja of Baroda.

Deva Dasis dancing Bharat Natyam, with four Nattuvans playing music. This troupe was maintained at the court of H.H. the Maharaja of Baroda.

Gujerat folk dance.
(*Baroda Museum,*
painted by Kanu Desai)

The author in a Bharat Natyam posture.

Royal Thai Ballet

Origin of the Dance

LEGEND TELLS HOW the dance came to earth as a gift of the gods, and when one sees the Royal Thai Ballet, one readily believes the legend, for such a scintillating spectacle of elegant and virile gestures, of noble bearing, of pathos and humor, reenacting the beloved tales of ancient kings, celestial beings, and heroes, is a credible invention of the gods.

Historically, the dance came to Thailand through the great Khmer Empire. Extinct a thousand years now, the superb ruins of the Khmer cities lay lost in the rampant forest until Henri Mouhot rediscovered them in 1860, and brought these amazing wonders to the attention of the world. Of all that splendid civilization, only one eyewitness has left a record. This record was found in Chinese archives. Tcheou Ta-kouan, a Chinese ambassador, visited the Khmer Empire at the height of its glory in the twelfth century and wrote a detailed account of the luxurious life he witnessed in Angkor Thom, the Khmer capital. Archaeological research and the lavishly sculptured walls of Angkor confirm Tcheou Ta-kouan's report.

When the Thai (Siamese) attacked and conquered the Khmer Empire (ancient Cambodia), they were themselves conquered by the beauty of Khmer arts. Among the 90,000 prisoners of war were artists and artisans whom the Thai carried home with them to embellish their capital. But of all the arts, it was especially the dance that the Thai loved and cultivated.

The dance had come to the Khmers with the Siva cult from India. Those great temples scattered through the forest for hundreds of miles were built to the glory of Siva. One of the temples supported, according to record, a ballet of 625, including musicians, since the dance played a

35

very important part in the Siva ritual. The kings, nobles, and provincial governors also had their private ballets for entertainments on festive occasions. When the purifying wave of Buddhism rolled over the land, the temple rituals were simplified and the dance excluded from religious services, but it continued at the courts, and probably each village had its local ballet as many do today. These ballets were, and still are, the theatre of the people. Dance dramas are the theatre and much more, for they contain the literature, the poetry, the history, the beloved myths and legends of a glorious past.

Although this dance art has a definitely prescribed technique, it has not remained static. From time to time some especially gifted artist makes contributions or innovations. During the reign of King Chulalongkorn some fifty years ago, His Royal Highness Prince Naris wrote new dance dramas and music, as did more recently Rama VI, King of Siam from 1911 to 1925. All the courtiers studied the dance and took part in the dance dramas.

In former times the dancers lived within the palace enclosure as part of the royal household, but in 1925 the palace budget was greatly reduced, so now the dancers live in their own homes, and go daily to their quarters in the palace enclosure where they are trained, rehearsed, fed, and paid a small salary by the government. In 1925 the royal troupe numbered 300 dancers and musicians. Today the royal troupe has been reduced, but it is still composed of the finest artists of the realm.

Characteristics of the Dance

From its original source, the dance filtered through the Khmers to the Thai, losing some forms, evolving others according to racial taste, until it became a distinctively Thai dance art. The extreme upward turning of the fingers is an example, a motif repeated in Thai roofs; in the shafts of water-buffalo carts; in the golden paintings on walls, furniture, and books; in the ear frames of the royal mongkots (headdresses) which are identical in form with those worn by dancers; in the epaulettes of ceremonial costumes of kings and princes, which are also identical with those worn by dancers representing these roles; and in numerous other ornamental details. This upward curve, or flourish, is characteristic of Thai art. Only in Khmer, Cambodian, and Thai dances is this extreme curvature of the fingers used. An uplifting of the toes and deeply flexed knees complete the plastic harmony of the dance postures.

Training for the Dance

In the Royal Palace at Bangkok, Thailand, I had the privilege of studying with Kunying Natakanuraksa, the Directress of the Royal Ballet. Her name means Titled or Noble Guardian of the Dance. Her husband, the late Phya Natakanurak, was a celebrated dancer, and for many years directed the Royal Ballet. He knew every role and every gesture in the extensive repertoire of the Thai classic dance. Kunying Natakan-uraksa ably carries on her husband's work, for she too knows every role, though when she taught me she was then a grandmother of sixty. When she begins to dance, she is instantly transformed by the magic of this art into whatever she desires to represent. The day she was teaching me the role of Nang-Ma-Tcha, the siren of the river Menam, she became, before the enchanted eyes of my pianist and myself, a seductive mermaid on a sandy riverbank. Then, entering the river with a gesture, she suddenly became a graceful fish with quivering fins, darting through the water, then poised looking here and there, slowly rising to the surface and darting off again, leaping and splashing like a dolphin in the transparent water of the perfectly dry studio. Her hands became fins, and her body supple and glinting as a fish. In another lesson she was Kinnari, the gorgeously plumed bird-woman, the celestial singer, flying leisurely through a tropical forest, flitting about the studio with birdlike glances on the lookout for luscious fruit to eat. For Mekala, the Lightning Goddess, Kunying became a serene and beautiful young goddess descending from her sky palace to dance in the clouds and gaze at the earth far beneath. In still another lesson, she transformed herself into Hanuman, the beloved white monkey of the Ramayana stories, crouching, impish, restless and scratching, leaping sud-denly, then pausing, head cocked while thinking of some new mischief. Kunying's hands became simian with hook-fingers and set-out thumb, and her very eyes became round, shiny black beads.

One day Kunying Natakanuraksa brought out a silk-wrapped book and laid it gently down; looked at me meaningfully and said, "Anjali." Anjali is the Thai word for the reverential salute to a great personage or to a sacred object. So Kunying and I knelt and bowed and made Anjali together before the book. There are only two such books in ex-istence: one in the Thai National Library, and this one in the possession of the Directress of the Royal Ballet.

Then Kunying opened the sacred book. It opens like a screen, black pages painted with gold figures of a man and a woman in dancing poses on each page. The names of the poses are written beneath in Thai. Here is the record of all the basic positions of the Thai dance. The gold lady and gentleman dance over the black pages in antique costumes, very rich, yet simple, which cling and flow with the dance movements: ethereal costumes in contrast to the heavy jeweled and brocaded costumes of today. But as the gilded ones dance in the book, so do the Thai dancers of today, and so did they long before the book was painted.

Training is begun very early, at three or four years of age. Children so young do not dance, but they sit and watch the others so that they grow up in the atmosphere of dance, and each day their small elbows, fingers, toes, and knees are exercised to attain that remarkable flexibility typical of Thai dance. Later, training consists mainly of following the older dancers. The stars lead, and the rest follow in order of merit. If a young dancer shows promise, the instructor places him or her behind a good dancer to follow the movements, the teacher correcting by touching the head, arms, elbows, fingers, or knees, and explaining the direction the eyes should take. In spite of a very rich technique and astonishing suppleness, there are no hours of *barre* work to undergo. However, to perfect a certain movement it will be repeated many times in succession and then in sequence with the preceding and succeeding movements until it has attained the required quality.

The most classic form of the Thai dance is called Khon, and is danced exclusively by male dancers, feminine parts being taken by the most slender and delicate-featured boys. The dances are dance dramas relating episodes from the Ramayana and Mahabharata epics, or Thai myths and historical episodes, always about kings and princesses, heroes, celestial beings, and wonderful mythological creatures, representing the ideal types of the race. Even the villains are ideal villains.

The second classic form is the Lakhon, danced by women or by both men and women, and relating the same dance dramas. The feminine style of dancing differs from the masculine only in a certain modesty of deportment. The feet are placed nearer togther, the knees are flexed toward the front instead of being widely opened to the sides, in a ballet second position, distinctly different from the masculine style. The head is carried modestly, chin slightly drawn in, eyes often downcast. All feminine movements are gentle. Movements and postures are otherwise identical.

The masculine style expresses virility and strength, especially in the roles of warriors, giants, and demons. The feet are placed widely apart in a ballet second position, knees are deeply flexed in *plié* or are raised hip-high; the transition movements from one pose to another are sharp and energetic; the head is carried high and arrogantly. Roles of refined or gentle masculine characters are played in a style somewhere between that of a virile warrior and the feminine style. Characters such as Hanuman, the White Monkey, are definitely comic roles, although sometimes scenes of touching pathos are played by such characters. When a clown plays pathetic incidents, they are the more poignant by contrast.

Costume for the Dance

The costumes for the Royal Ballet are kept in a special wardrobe building in the palace enclosure. It has whitewashed walls and a barred and locked door, and stands among the buildings prescribed for the dance. Inside, the wardrobe building looks like a museum with its center cases for jewelry and accessories, wall cases for hanging garments and headdresses, drawers and shelves for precious brocades which are kept rolled, not folded. Each case is carefully locked, since the contents have considerable value.

As one enters the cool, white-plastered building from the heat and glare outside, one has the impression of entering a fairyland cave; jeweled headdresses sparkle and twinkle; masks glower, smirk impishly, or stare in surprise; garments of rich colored silks, pailletted velvets, and gold and silver brocades glow with soft radiance; on the floor stands a chariot such as seen in ancient sculptures, with ornaments that repeat the upward Thai flourish; horse heads of leather for the dancers who draw the chariot stand near; painted wings and tails for Kinnara and Kinnari, the celestial singers, are here too, made of buffalo hide, gilded, painted, and encrusted with little flashing mirrors; tails for mermaids and many other evocative objects glint from the cases. In former times the dancers wore real jewels, but these often fell from their settings during performances, so imitation jewelry was substituted, beautifully made and still quite expensive. Each role has its typical costume, distinguished by details of ornament and color.

The basic feminine costume consists of a tight-fitting underjacket with very short sleeves; a panung (skirt) which is a rectangle of beautiful material about forty inches wide and three yards long, of brocaded silk, or silver or gold brocade, drawn about the hips, with the extra length being pleated in front and held by a belt; a broad velvet cape, pailletted and jeweled, which is fastened to the belt in front and hangs behind nearly as long as the panung; a broad jeweled collar, armlets, bracelets, rings; a tchedah (headdress) of gilded buffalo hide, studded with tiny mirrors, denoting the role of the danseuse.

The basic male costume consists of knee-length trousers over which is draped the panung, the extra length being twisted into a roll, passed through the legs, and tucked into the belt behind; an embroidered panel which hangs in front from the belt, and two more which hang over each thigh; a tight, long-sleeved jacket with up-curved epaulettes; a broad, jeweled collar with two chains crossing on the back and on the breast; a tchedah, which, like the female dancer's headdress, indicates the role being played.

The value of the costumes varies with their richness, but the most expensive is that of Rama or of Tosakan which in 1938 cost about 4,000 ticals or $2,000.

Masks and Makeup

The picturesque old artist, Nai Siri Yanthanaphon, who makes the masks, wings, tails, headdresses, and other accoutrements for the Royal Ballet, was making a tchedah for me. His humble house was at the end of a narrow stone walk leading from a street door so inconspicuous that no one but a frequent visitor would ever notice it. But this modest dwelling, whose roof was so low that a person not more than five feet six in height could just manage to stand in it, was a fairyland laboratory. Pots of paint and gold lacquer stood about, and masks and tchedahs in various stages of construction were perched here and there, some already twinkling with little mirrors encrusted in their gold-lacquered surfaces.

The first time I visited Nai Siri Yanthanaphon, he did not measure my head for the tchedah, but instead measured my hand and assured me he could make a headdress for anyone, even in a faraway land, to fit his head just from the hand measurement. Now, a tchedah must really fit perfectly, because if it is not just right, it is quite uncomfortable, even painful, to wear, pinching the head, causing headaches and faintness; or if too loose, giving an insecure, top-heavy sensation that may cause the dancer to lose balance. The day I went for my tchedah, it went on my head, but pinched here, was too loose there, and did not frame my face properly. I did not look at all like the ravishing goddess into which I had expected to be transformed. Evidently my proportions of head and hand did not correspond to the Thai, and as I was the first foreigner Nai Siri had ever made a tchedah for, he had to abandon his tradition and measure my head for a new tchedah. So he asked me with a polite and friendly smile if he might touch my head to measure it. The head is sacred in Thailand, and no one would dare to touch the head of another person. Even Kunying Natakanuraksa asked my permission to touch my head to correct it in dance positions. What a difference from lands where "a good sock on the jaw," "a punch on the nose," or the call to "knock his teeth out," "slap him down," and *"foutre une paire de claques"* are everyday expressions and actions!

Masks are used for all character roles, such as hermits, saints, holy men, yakshas, ogres, Devatas (celestial beings), Hanuman and other monkey roles. Only feminine roles and the gentle princes are without masks, but their faces are painted white and kept impassive during the dance so that the impersonal effect of a mask is attained. The mask and accompanying headdress are made in one unit, put on and taken off together. The features of the masks are often exaggerated to enhance expression, and are painted elaborately in traditional colorings. A yaksha's mask, for example, is always jade-green with round, bulging eyes and fang teeth. A Devata mask is pink with elongated, dreamy eyes and a gently smiling mouth.

Facial makeup is simple. Faces are whitened with water paint, not the greasepaint traditional to Western actors; eyebrows are painted in the approved arch with black; and lips are painted red. All the characteristics of masks and makeup in both the Thai and Cambodian dances are the same.

One realizes the height of corporeal expression has been attained when seeing these actor-dancers playing the whole gamut of human emotion without the aid of facial expressions. The eloquence of their art must be seen to be fully understood and appreciated.

Dance Properties

The various roles have special dance properties that accompany them. A prince or king carries a rod about 27 inches long, encrusted with tiny diamond-shaped mirrors that flash when it is twirled during the dance. Ravana (or Tosakan as he is called in Thailand) carries a tapering, curved cane finished by a Thai ornament at the upper end which is flourished during his dance. Sometimes he appears with a fan. Hanuman often carries a three-pronged instrument similar to a trident. The Thunder God, Ramasoun, wields a clublike accessory encrusted with little mirrors.

Women's roles sometimes require flowers carried in the hands. Mekala, the Lightning Goddess, appears with her "lightning-maker," a small mirror-studded sphere which creates lightning-like flashes during the dance. Nang-Ma-Tcha, the River Goddess, wears a fishtail; and Kinnari and

Kinnara (female and male celestial singers) wear wings and elaborate tails.

In accordance with each story, chariots and animals—horses, elephants, and others—may be used; but the most indispensable property, one which is always present, is the tiang, a low table-like platform representing a throne, a bed, a seat, a palace, a house, or whatever the story requires.

Scenery is nonexistent but is evoked in the minds of the spectators by the acting of the dancers and the unfolding of the dance dramas. Recently some attempts have been made to introduce scenery in the European sense. The results were "realistic" in the best Late Victorian style, quite out of harmony with the evocative qualities of the dance dramas. It is to be hoped that the use of garishly painted set pieces of canvas and wood will be discontinued or improved to correspond with the spirit of the dance.

Music for the Dance

Thai music has a history of more than a thousand years. Its tradition has been carried on orally and by memory; no notation existed. The National Library has conserved an ancient list of Thai musical pieces, recorded by their names, but of these more than half have been lost forever, being unknown by living musicians. In view of this misfortune, His Royal Highness, Prince Damrong, in 1929 requested Phra Chen Duriyanga to devise a notation system to record and conserve Thai traditional music. Phra Chen Duriyanga, who had studied Western music, made a thorough study of Thai music and the technique of playing the instruments, and devised a means of recording the Thai musical modes in Western notation.

Thai music is not derived from any other system of music such as Chinese or Javanese, as is sometimes supposed, but is purely Thai. The scale has seven full tones arranged equidistantly. It is a diatonic scale, neither major nor minor in the Western musical sense, but a typically Thai diatonic scale. The Thai orchestra is called the Pi-Phat orchestra, and its instruments are all percussion with the exception of the pi, the flute. They are:

ranad ek: an alto xylophone of wood or bamboo; 21 resonance bars.
ranad thume: a bass xylophone of wood; 17 resonance bars.
ranad thong ek: alto xylophone of brass or steel; 21 resonance bars.
ranad thong thume: bass xylophone of brass or steel; 17 resonance bars.
gong wong yai: 16 small bronze gongs in a circular frame.
gong wong lek: like the gong wong yai but pitched one octave higher.
tapone: a horizontal drum, both ends having drumheads.

song na: like the tapone but smaller and held on the lap of player.

klong thad: a large, vertical drum; always used in twos or threes, each having a different pitch.

gong hooi: a set of 3, 5, or 7 gongs hung in a frame.

charb lek: a pair of small cymbals.

charb yai: a pair of large cymbals.

ching: a pair of small cup-shaped cymbals of fine resonance. They are the time beater and timekeeper of the Pi-Phat orchestra. They set the pace for the whole performance. There is no conductor in a Pi-Phat or any other Thai orchestra.

mong: a single medium-sized gong, used only for sound effects.

krub sebha: two bars of hardwood used to mark time during recitations, although these may be replaced by the ching.

pi nai: a flute made of rosewood.

To approximate Thai with Western instruments, substitute for the:

ranad ek: a treble wood xylophone

ranad thume: an alto-wood xylophone or marimba

ranad thong ek: a treble steel xylophone

ranad thong thume: an alto steel xylophone

gong wong yai: a glockenspiel or Resonophone

gong wong lek: a celesta

tapone: no equivalent

song na: no equivalent

klong thad: timpani

gong hooi: no equivalent

charb lek: small cymbals

charb yai: large cymbals

ching: triangle

mong: gong

The role of the gong wong yai (glockenspiel) is to carry the principal melody. The ranad ek (treble xylophone) usually produces variations on the principal melody. The ranad thume and ranad thong thume embroider freely on the principal melody. The gong wong lek (celesta) sometimes duplicates the principal melody, at times creates variations on it. The gongs are used for special sound effects. The ching are extremely important. They are the time beaters and timekeepers of the orchestra. Their clear resonance gives two sounds: alternately: "ching-chap," the long ringing sound and the muted sound marking the up- and down-beats of the music. The ching are the conductor of the Pi-Phat orchestra.

The method of tuning the ranads and the gongs is interesting. The wood or bamboo bars are of graduated lengths and thicknesses, but humidity and temperature alter the tone. To tune the ranads and gongs, beeswax mixed with scraped lead is heated slightly and placed in a lump on the underside of each resonance bar of the ranads or the inside rim of the gongs, in larger or smaller amounts until the exact pitch or tone is attained. All the instruments are played traditionally resting on the floor, which gives them an increased resonance.

Since the Thai dance is dance drama, moments occur when both speaking and gestures are used to tell the story. At such times a narrator begins to recite the story, synchronizing his words with the dance gestures. As the Thai do not like the beauty of the words to be confused with or distorted to fit the music, the musicians cease to play when the human voice begins. The krub-sebha or ching continue marking the time with their sharp but melodious sounds. As the narrator approaches the end of his recitation, the ranads begin softly to play, and when he finishes, all the instruments again accompany the dance. This is a distinctively Thai innovation. It is accomplished smoothly, with no break or interruption, and gives the decided advantage of hearing the poetic beauty of the words clearly so that they may be fully appreciated. Moreover, the effect of having the music fade in and fade out intensifies immensely the dramatic effect.

As in Indian music, there are modes to express the various sentiments, emotions, and actions. The Thai Department of Fine Arts has a list of over 1,200 melodies. They are divided into 36 groups, each for a particular purpose, such as: 13 melodies for expressing anger; 21 for sorrow or affliction; 4 for joy; 7 for reflection; meditation, contemplation; 4 for excitement; and many others. A choreographer chooses a story and then selects from these musical modes the melodies for his dance drama. Appropriate variations may be introduced as desired. The meanings of the musical themes are so well known to the Thai people that a blind person hearing the music would be able to understand clearly the action of the drama being played.

Thai music is a source of great national pride. It has the same fairyland quality that exists in other Thai arts, the same feeling of the uplifting flourish that is seen in roof lines, in dancers' fingers, in ornamental details. It is "happy music," rippling and cascading like a crystal mountain stream, at times throbbing like the sea or tinkling like the little wind-bells that hang from the edges of temple roofs, at times as serene as the face of Buddha. It is reposeful, soothing, or exciting, but always melodic and delightful to the ear.

Presentation of the Dance

In addition to all the places one might expect to find dance performances—at the Royal Court, in public theatres, on little temporary stages in the midst of public gatherings—one of the occasions in Thailand for the presentation of a Khon ballet is at cremations. The Thai are Buddhists, and cremate their dead, and one of the most important features of the cremation of a notable or wealthy person is the dancing of a Khon ballet in an open-air theatre especially erected for it. The Thai take the logical attitude that the departure of a loved one from this life to a happier one should be a joyful event and therefore an occasion for feasting and entertainment.

A Dance Rehearsal

The dance rehearsal hall in the Royal Palace enclosure is a large pavilion, a Thai roof supported on tall, slender columns over an excellent dance floor. It is entirely open on three sides with a wall closing the fourth side. The crenelated outer wall of the palace enclosure has an obscure rear door guarded by an armed soldier. Through this unpretentious entrance we arrive at the generously proportioned dance pavilion, set in a grove of banana trees, where, on this particular day, the Ballet is rehearsing for the coming Thai New Year celebration. The King of the Giants, kneeling on the traditional dance platform, the tiang, is miming with high-spirited gestures to his followers who are kneeling in attentive rows before him. At one side stands a man with a book, reciting in rhythmic verse what the Yaksha King says in gesture. The beauty of the man's voice in quality, diction, and dramatic feeling is remarkable. Some forty boys and young men sit in groups along the side of the pavilion, waiting their turn to rehearse. One or two soloists work in a corner on special dance sequences under the keen eyes of one of the masters. Two small boys, working on one of the monkey roles, clutch one of the columns supporting the roof and execute a difficult leg movement, stamping in rhythm and raising their legs alternately no fewer than 500 times until their tired muscles cramp. Only then does their master permit them to rest. Training is exacting and severe. Kunying Natakanuraksa meanwhile goes about among the group that is dancing, correcting their postures, touching them here or there —the angle of the arm, a little more acute; legs in deeper *plié*; torso straighter, weight more to right or left; chin higher; head in sharper profile—a constant striving for perfect form and line.

A group of teachers and singers sits on a mat at the left, around a tray of lovely silver objects composing a betel-chewing set: bowls large and small, little jars, and other objects, all of pure silver and most beautifully engraved. The forms of these objects are so intriguing that one is tempted to take up betel-chewing just for the pleasure of using them.

A Performance of the Royal Ballet

At the Thai New Year in March, 1938, the Royal Ballet danced a Khon two nights in succession, on a specially erected stage in the great square before the Royal Palace, for the entertainment of the general public. It was the high point of the New Year festivities and the performances, which began at seven in the evening, lasted until after midnight.

In the dressing room behind the dance platform, the men and boys were being made up with water paint. Stiff, richly brocaded costumes were being folded and pleated on the dancers and tugged and pulled to make them hang just right. Finally the dancers were sewn into them. It was a very warm night, and the process of getting painted, dressed, and sewed into the costumes was a long one, but no one was cross or ill-tempered for the dance is a divine gift, is reverenced, and to dance is an honor. For proof of reverence, one has only to note the altar in the dressing room whereon are placed the traditional hermit's mask, the mongkot (ceremonial headdress for royalty), flowers, incense, pure water, and a burning candle. At this altar each actor, before donning his final jewels and headdress, prays for a moment with clasped hands.

When the music began, the public, standing two hundred feet deep on all three sides of the platform, was waiting with upturned, expectant faces. There was no place left for me, so Kunying pushed me onto the very stage where I sat on the floor, huddled in a corner among a group of Thai children for more than five hours, to watch, entranced, the dénouement of a heroic tale of giants and monkeys, of princes, princesses, and Devatas, of warriors and trusting friends and of sly enemies who resorted to magic forces to attain their wicked ends.

The story was revealed through the most complex and skillful interweaving of group action separated by solo dances, duos, and trios. The choreography never repeated itself but always presented new groupings, perspectives, and stage pictures. Scenery there was none, light effects were nonexistent—only white floods were used—nor did one feel the lack of them, for the dancers themselves with their dance properties were the scenery, and the costumes of dazzling richness that glowed or flashed brilliantly in rapid movements were the light effects.

A long sequence of scenes like those intriguing Thai frescoes illustrating episodes from the Ramayana and Mahabharata were acted, one linking with another without a break: the joyful meeting of two friends, both princes; bad news brought by one of them; the preparation for battle; the sortie in war chariots in gallant but risky postures like those of the sculptured kings at Angkor; arrival at the enemy camp; a conference—the dancers were panting now in the heat of the night, and those bowing low before their general as he planned the attack, took advantage of the moment to turn their faces from the audience, raise their masks slightly, and gasp a few breaths of sultry air before they were off again into combat to capture Rama; the grief and consternation of the monkeys as they searched excitedly for Rama whom they loved, and consulted among themselves in a rapid chattering dialogue spoken by the narrators accompanying the scene; the encounter of Hanuman with his son by Nang-Ma-Tcha, the River Goddess whom he once loved (Hanuman's son acted like a monkey and fish combined, showing his two lineages, a clever and difficult piece of acting. There was fine play of tenderness and grief in this meeting of Hanuman with his son); a descent into the depths of a lake via the stem of a giant lotus; an interview with a Devata to request supernatural aid; and the grand finale when the villain, riding an elephant, was at last destroyed by magic power. The triumph of Good over Evil—the same ideal in all lands.

Dance Technique

See Royal Cambodian Dances chapter, under Dance Technique.

Dance Exercises

See Royal Cambodian Dances chapter, under Dance Exercises.

Concluding Thoughts

Western people, with their matter-of-fact way of thinking, invariably want to know what part such a highly cultivated and ancient art plays in modern national culture, what it really means to people of Thailand today. The answer, I believe, is revealed in the following incidents.

The train in which I was crossing Thailand stopped at a tiny station in the rice fields. Presently, I heard two high, clear little voices saying, "Anjali! Anjali!" That lovely ancient word of greeting I knew from my dance studies. But way off here in the rice fields—what could it mean? Curiously I looked from the train window to see two small girls smiling and saluting me with the classical Anjali, their small palms pressed together, their fingers opening like flower petals. Such a charming gesture should be rewarded, so I handed them a tin of salmon from my lunch basket, and have hoped ever since that they or their peasant parents knew how to open it.

One sunny day in Bangkok I was looking at some antique jewelry in a quiet store. Suddenly the atmosphere became a-quiver with hushed excitement. Then I noticed that a big black limousine had drawn up before the shop, a liveried footman had opened the door, and several delicate little old ladies dressed in grays and lavenders were descending. The shop-keeper hurriedly brought out a dainty gold chair, and stood ceremoniously to place it for one of the ladies. As she sat upon it, the others grouped themselves about her, some with fans behind her, others sitting attentively at her feet, on the floor. And they sat just as I had been taught in the dance: the identical placement of the legs, body, arms, and head! It was too wonderful—here before my very eyes a real ballet with a real Queen surrounded by her ladies-in-waiting! For it was King Chulalongkorn's last Queen, a widow now for many years, come to inspect some rare old pieces of jewelry which the jeweler now brought out for Her Majesty.

Shortly after my arrival in Bangkok, I attended a Thai theatre with Prince Sokol and his daughter. Presently a dancer appeared, and to my delight, Prince Sokol began to relate to me in running narrative the story the dancer was telling in gestures. As the gestures succeeded one another, the Prince's narrative developed into a captivating story, and I learned that every Thai can "read" the classic dance in this way.

On a café terrace in Paris, some months later, I was lunching with two Thai gentlemen. We talked of the Thai dance, and I asked them to name various speaking-gestures which I demonstrated. As they gave me the names, they delightedly exclaimed over meeting someone so far from their home who understood and loved their art.

On a visit to London, I had occasion to call at the Thailand Embassy. In the salon were a number of Thai bronzes of dancing figures. The Ambassador responded to my interest with an enthuasiastic discourse on Thai dance which lasted until he accompanied me to the door for my departure.

In Thailand, advertisements of modern products carry motifs taken from Thai mythology and classic dance art. Labels for cloth have the seal of Mekala and Ramasoun, the Lightning Goddess and the Thunder God; paper jackets for phonograph records are ornamented with a design of Thai celestial musicians sitting in the clouds with their instruments; figures of Kinnara and Kinnari, the celestial mythological singers, ornament the modern lampposts along Bangkok's most modern Avenue Rajadamnoen; Thai airmail stamps bear the design of Garuda. What more appropriate design could have been chosen than the strong wings of the benevolent, mythological eagle? Garuda is also the protector of mankind, and his figure is the seal and the coat of arms of Thailand. These forms are used because the people have an emotional response to them. The Thai identify with these symbols because they love and understand them.

These few illustrations show that the manners and customs represented in the dance are still, as they have been since ancient times, a living part of daily life. The stories the dance dramas tell form a most important part of the national literature. The costumes worn by the dancers are the same as the ceremonial dress of courtiers and of royalty itself. The music is known and understood by all. The whole art is a synthesis of life from remote times which still pulsates through the life of today. The Thai nation takes the greatest pride in its dance as the mirror of its racial spirit.

A page from the
Thai Dance Book.

Kunying Natakanuraksa,
Directress of the
Royal Thai Ballet.

Nai Siri Yanthanaphon,
the Royal Thai Ballet's mask-maker.

A golden Kinnara in Vat Pra Keo, Bangkok, Thailand

A temple in Vat Pra Keo, Bangkok, Thailand

Crocodile Lady in Vat Pra Keo, Bangkok, Thailand

Temple guardians, Bangkok, Thailand

Kunying Natakanuraksa as Mekala looking from her sky-palace. Rehearsal hall of the Royal Thai Ballet in the background.

A small Hanuman, son of a famous dancer.

"Mosquitoes" in the Royal Thai Ballet.

Members of the Royal Thai Ballet pose for the author.

Xenia Zarina as Mekala, Goddess of Lightning, demonstrating the speaking gestures: "I . . . shall go there," and the feminine sitting position.
(*photo by Noutiyal, Mussoorie, India*)

Xenia Zarina
as Mekala,
Goddess of Lightning
(Thai mythology).

Xenia Zarina as a Kinnari, demonstrating position of looking or searching for something—hands in hamsasya mudra.

(photos by Noutiyal, Mussoorie, India)

As Nang-Ma-Tcha, Goddess of the Menam River. Hands in pataka mudra represent fish fins.

Demonstrating Anjali in kneeling position on the tiang.

Xenia Zarina in classic Thai dance costume representing a princess or a goddess.

(*photos by* Semo, Mexico)

Hands in Anjali (salutation); feet in "flying" posture.

Hands in hamsasya represent an offering of flowers; feet in "flying" posture.

Closeup of headdress; hands in anjali
(salutation)
(*photo by Semo, Mexico*)

Royal Cambodian Dances

Cambodian History

THE CAMBODIANS proudly claim descent from the great Khmer Empire, and their arts and customs are a continuation of that brilliant culture. The Western world knew nothing of the Khmer civilization until the dramatic discovery of Angkor by Henri Mouhot in 1860. Since then, French archaeologists, working assiduously, have recovered valuable information and found numerous marvelous sites of temples, palaces, and cities scattered through the Cambodian forest.

The Khmer civilization seems to have sprung rather suddenly into glorious bloom, and continuing for several centuries, disappeared as mysteriously as it had appeared. The natives of the Cambodian forest say the gods built these vast, elaborate cities. Certain it is that very unusual minds conceived, planned, and directed the construction of these architectural and engineering wonders. Scattered over hundreds of miles of rampant tropical forest lie the remains of cities, reservoirs, canals, palaces, and temples. Angkor Thom (Angkor City), the last great Khmer city, had a population of over a million, an impressive number for any city a thousand years ago. The numerous cities were not all coexistent, but succeeded each other during the centuries as Khmer urban needs changed. A valuable key in determining their historical dates is the artistic evolution of their buildings. Following the Thai attack in the thirteenth and four-

teenth centuries against the Khmer Empire, a series of wars ensued until all
Cambodia fell under Siamese influence where it remained until 1863 when
it became a French protectorate, part of Indo-Chine Française, independent
of Siam. Cambodia now had its own king again, and Pnompenh became
the capital.

Character of the Dance

The sculptured walls of the Khmer cities decaying in the forest testify
to the place the dance held in that civilization. There are literally thousands
of carved dance scenes: religious ritual dances, court dances, dancers at play
in a garden, celestial dances, as well as decorative friezes of dancing girls
(Apsarases), and Tevadas or Devatas (celestial beings), standing serenely
in their niches with enigmatic smiles on their lovely sensuous faces. The
Bayon (temple of Siva) in Angkor Thom has a wall carved with one
especially intriguing scene: a large panel representing the daily life of
court dancers. Amid luxuriant vegetation in a closed garden, the dancers
are bathing, arranging their hair, being massaged, exercising, and playing.
A point to remark is that all these thousands of sculptured dancers are
always female. I did not see a single representation of a male dancer in
any of the ruins I visited in and around Angkor. This is accounted for by
the fact that the Khmer temples were dedicated to Siva and Vishnu (later
to Buddhism) and these two cults employed girl dancers (Deva Dasis) in
the temple ceremonies, a tradition still observed in South India today. The
Court dancers were undoubtedly part of the "harem" of the king or
noble, as they are to this day in the Royal Palace of Cambodia. The Royal
Ballet is, in fact, under the absolute direction of the king's first wife.

Since the dance played such an important part in Khmer life, it is
reasonable to suppose that even the great disaster that made them abandon
their sumptuous cities could not entirely destroy their beloved dance art.
The Siva cult still needed ritual dances, and kings and courtiers still
craved the diversion of the dance, for it was much more than mere entertainment. They carried the dance with them wherever they fled, and
preserved it tenaciously. When they settled again under Siamese rule,
Cambodian kings and princes became local governors, and maintained
their private ballets as they still do today. As in the past, the ballets are
always composed of women dancers. This is remarkable since in Japan,
China, Java, Bali, and Thailand it is always the men who are the great

actors and dancers, who carry on the most classic traditions of the dance drama. In certain lands and epochs, women have been entirely banned from appearing in theatrical entertainments. In Thailand, which shares the same cultural heritage as Cambodia, the most classic form of the dance, the Khon, is always danced by men. The explanation of this Cambodian dance phenomenon opens a trail leading back to ancient India with its traditions and customs relating to the dance.

In 1937 George Groslier was director of the lovely Albert Sarraut Museum at Pnompenh. A distinguished artist, painter, writer, and connoisseur of Cambodian arts who has done invaluable work for Cambodia, M. Groslier has also written and illustrated a splendid book, *Danseuses Cambodgiennes*. He arranged for me to have lessons with Princess Say Sang Van, the favorite dancer in the Royal Ballet. She was married to the brother of the King of Cambodia, but after domestic disagreements, she left the court. The French Colonial Government had for some time been in an embarrassing position: the fame and beauty of the Cambodian dances had spread to Europe, and now distinguished visitors came to visit Cambodia and wanted to see the dances. They had made a long and difficult journey, and the Cambodian dancers were a strong drawing card. The French Colonial Government could not ask the King to produce the Royal Ballet, which was part of his royal household, just to please strangers he had never heard of. So the visitors most often had to leave Cambodia disappointed in their hope of seeing the Cambodian ballet. Now Princess Say Sang Van was just the solution to the problem. The French were delighted by her change in social position, and were quick to endow her to organize a ballet trained in the court tradition which would be available to the French Colonial Government when needed. This meant security for the Princess and satisfaction for the visitors, as well as new stimulation of Cambodian dance art. But for this happy circumstance, I would have had the utmost difficulty in studying Cambodian dance. As it was, it took half my energy to have even irregular lessons. Often I would go on the appointed day only to find that the Princess and the whole ballet had vanished. The servant did not speak any French, and explained to me by waving his hands in the air. Presumably the ballet had flown off to other regions, like the carved Apsarases at Angkor where whole ballets soar joyously across the skies, arms and feet daintily raised in the "flying" pose. Then, suddenly, the Princess and ballet would reappear and my lessons would continue until the next "flight."

Training for the Dance

Cambodian and Thai dance training and technique are identical to those set forth in the chapter on Royal Thai Ballet. The Royal Cambodian Ballet recruits in a number of ways: a pretty child may be offered by her parents; a provincial governor may send a lovely child as his offering to the king's ballet; or when provincial ballets come to dance before the king on such festive occasions as the king's birthday, an attractive little dancer may be noticed and asked for. New pupils, being accepted into the Royal Ballet, are appraised as to type by the teachers, and assigned to roles suitable to them. The following is a quotation from *Danses Cambodgiennes* by His Excellency Samdach Chaufea Veang Thiounn who was Prime Minister at the time of my visit to Cambodia, and an ardent devotee of the Cambodian dance.

"Training is begun in classes of a dozen, and lessons are at a very early hour, while the dew is still on the plants in the palace gardens. The dew is used to massage the joints, to aid suppleness in articulation of elbows and wrists, fingers, knees and toes. When the new pupils have been limbered sufficiently and have learned some of the dance movements, they enter class with the older dancers.

"Samdach Preas Kron is the genie of the dance, and every lesson is preceded by a ceremony called 'Sampas Kron.' It is a salute to the genius of the dance and to the dance mistress. The dance mistress sits beside the altar in the rehearsal room, and each pupil brings an offering of betel leaves, candles, incense sticks, perfumed water, and bouquets of flowers. The pupil places the offerings before the mistress, and performs the ritual salute, 'Anjali.' The teacher then wishes the pupil success, and pours some of the perfumed water on her head.

"The pupils are then grouped according to roles, and each group works separately. They dance without music or song. The mistress strikes the floor with a rod to give the rhythm, and with the rod corrects the pupils' positions or points out mistakes."

Every lesson begins with all the pupils dancing together the "slow tempo," a series of movements and poses of about twenty minutes' duration. This is followed by another series in "fast tempo." These two series might be compared to the "groundwork" of a ballet class, since they are training for timing, balance, and perfection of posture. After this, the rehearsal of a dance drama begins with miming of roles, solos, and group action.

To quote again from His Excellency's book: "After months of practice, when the pupils have learned faultlessly the miming of their roles, the steps, postures, and movements, they are ready for the important ceremony, 'Pithi Sampeas Kron Lakhon Krop Muk,' which is the graduation ceremony. Thursday is the day sacred to Sampeas Preas Kron, so a Thursday of a fasting month is chosen for the graduation. Eight little altars are raised in the rehearsal hall with offerings upon them of flowers, betel, rice, incense, and perfumed water. Ten bonzes, the yellow-robed Buddhist priests, come to say prayers which are repeated by teachers and pupils. The following day, dance masks, headdresses, tiaras, toilet articles, makeup, flowers, and platters of food are placed on a white covered platform in the rehearsal hall. Musicians take their places, candles and incense are lit. A dignitary reads the invocation to Sampeas Preas Kron, the genius of the Dance. Pupils lift the platters of offerings onto their heads, and offer them to the four cardinal points. The dignitary dons the mask of the Anchorite, and places on the heads of the pupils the masks and headdresses distinctive to the roles in which they have been trained; sprinkles them with holy water; places a thread dipped in holy water on their shoulders; puts rice powder on their faces, perfume on their foreheads; and finally wishes them each good luck and happiness. The pupils, after this consecration, remove the masks and headdresses, and dance by groups; then, again donning the headdresses and masks, they dance a complete ballet. Now they, who were yesterday only pupils, have become authorized dancers with the insignia of their ancient art."

This elaborate ceremony takes place inside the Royal Palace. At Princess Say Sang Van's, the same ceremony in simpler form is enacted. My own lessons were accomplished thus: After watching the ballet practice in slow and fast tempos, and rehearse dances or a ballet dance drama for a coming performance, I had a private lesson in slow tempo, in fast tempo, and in excerpts from dances and miming. The Prima Ballerina danced and I followed, Madame Say Sang Van following me and correcting my positions as I danced. This was an excellent system, and I learned rapidly in a short time. Later the Princess invited me to follow the dancers during their rehearsals. This was extremely interesting and valuable as training, for I suddenly found myself part of a group, coordinating my movements with theirs and with the music. The Prima Ballerina was an exquisite dancer, kind and helpful as well. We became very good friends although we could hardly converse. I could understand and speak only a few words of Cambodian; she, who had gone to Paris to dance in the Colonial

Exposition of 1931, knew about as much French as I knew Cambodian. However, the dance is an international language, and we understood each other perfectly in that. After my lesson, at Princess Say Sang Van's request, I would demonstrate and teach her and the Prima Ballerina classic European ballet.

A candle and incense are always lit at the beginning of a lesson and rehearsal, and burn on until the lesson is over. The dances are recorded in precious handwritten books, some of them very old, and kept wrapped in fine silks and brocades. These books are never opened without the ceremonial salute, the Anjali, being made before them.

The royal dancers live in the palace enclosure and never leave it except on certain occasions or by special permission, since they form part of the royal household, but Madame Say Sang Van's ballet of eighteen dancers lives in her house. They are much freer than the palace dancers, and even go shopping at times. While not dancing or rehearsing, they make themselves useful in other ways: caring for the house and garden and making new costumes. One day when I arrived for a lesson, several were working at frames, sewing pure gold beads in ancient patterns onto velvet for new scarf-capes. The Princess showed me a small but heavy package of pure yellow-gold beads, and complained how expensive they had become. The dancers also flex each other, bending back fingers, wrists, elbows, and toe joints. The fingers are turned back nearly to touch the forearm, although in actual dance so extreme a flexation is never used, just as ballet dancers execute certain stretching exercises in the studio that they never show on the stage, for aesthetic reasons. When a dancer becomes old or incapacitated, she may retire to her former home, or remain in the palace as teacher or wardrobe mistress.

The Royal Ballet traditionally has been composed of 8 ballet mistresses, 108 dancers, 2 comic mimes (the only masculine elements in the ballet), 2 teachers of singing, 2 first singers, 2 readers, 24 choristers, 12 dressers, 4 guardians of jewels and costumes, 9 male musicians, and two *chefs d'orchestre* who are also considered part of the Royal Ballet.

As already mentioned, regional governors sometimes maintain their own ballets. There are also some small troupes in different localities of local girls trained by a retired palace dancer, who dance for Cambodian festivals. The life of these dancers is quite different from that of the royal dancers. They live in towns or villages, and engage freely in any occupation usual for a Cambodian woman. Some are even married. Their repertoire is the same as that of the royal dancers, but the technique is naturally less fine and the costumes less beautiful and expensive. As in all lands and at all times, there are also itinerant troupes.

In Cambodia, the classic dance is called Lakhon and is the same as the Thai Lakhon, the classic dance performed by women. Dance mistresses are also called Lakhons. Th.-B. van Lelyveld, in his book on Javanese dance, quotes a statement that Thai are engaged to teach the dance to the Royal Cambodian ballet. This is often true, for the dance is brilliantly preserved in Thailand, and is practiced and understood more thoroughly than in Cambodia. On pages 39 and 40 of his book *La Danse dans le Théâtre Javanais* he makes, however, several statements regarding the Cambodian dance that are inexact. Javanese dance does not "resemble" Cambodian dance, but is vastly different. Further, Cambodian dancers have no *marche à grands pas* like the Javanese actor-dancers, and they do not wear a sarong for the dance or in daily life. The sarong is a Malay garment, worn exclusively by Malay peoples in the Malay States, Sumatra, Java, and all of Indonesia, Thailand, and Cambodia. But native Cambodians and Cambodian dancers wear the sampot or the panung, a garment different in size, pattern, and manner of wearing.

Costume for the Dance

The woman's basic costume is:

A tightly fitting underjacket with no right arm sleeve, and a very short left arm sleeve, cut in a diagonal line from left shoulder to right armpit.

A sampot (skirt) of handwoven silk brocade or silk and silver or gold brocade. The sampot is about $3\frac{1}{2}$ yards long by $1\frac{1}{4}$ yards wide. It is held tightly about the hips, the two ends in front being pleated to the body, given a twist, the right end tucked securely into a cord tied tightly around the waist, the left end hanging out in a fan shape formed by the pleats; a broad scarf thrown over the left shoulder, hanging down behind. It is attached under the right arm. This scarf is of velvet, sewn with gold beads and tiny mirrors in traditional patterns. It is lined with a contrasting colored silk.

A collar of silver or gold plaques.

An ornament hanging from the neck onto the breast.

Several gold chains hanging from the left shoulder to the right hip.

A mokot (headdress for princess or goddess roles) gold-lacquered and set with tiny mirrors.

A tassel of champaka flowers and jasmine hanging from the mokot at one
side of the face.

An armlet on the right upper arm, bracelets on both wrists, bracelet of
jasmine flowers on the left wrist, silver or gold anklets on the ankles.

This is the costume for the leading feminine roles. Minor feminine
roles require similar but less elaborate costumes, and with alterations of
the mokot, sometimes only a tiara, and a scarf-cape covering both shoulders
as described under Thai feminine costume.

Masculine costumes are identical with Thai masculine costumes described in the chapter on Royal Thai Ballet.

The Royal Ballet has mokots and jewels set in pure gold for the leading
roles. Other ballets usually cannot afford more than silver gilt for the
leading roles. In 1937 a prince's costume cost about 8,000 piastres ($2,000)
and a princess' costume cost about 5,000 piastres for the King of Cambodia's
ballet.

Masks and Makeup

These have been described in the chapter on Royal Thai Ballet.

Dance Properties

Dance properties are the same as those described under Thai .dance
properties.

Music for the Dance

All I have said about Thai music applies also to Cambodian music. It
is delicate, dreamy, with the silvery, fluid sound of running water. It
creates an aerial, celestial atmosphere eminently pleasing to the ear and
to the imagination. When heard on a starry, jasmine-scented Cambodian
night, played in a distant temple, it is a potent opiate.

The orchestra that accompanies the dance is called Pi-Phat and the
instruments composing it are listed by His Excellency Thiounn as:

sralay or *pi:* flute (from which the orchestra derives its name)

roneat ek: a bamboo alto xylophone played by two small wooden hammers *roneat thung:* a hardwood basso xylophone

roneat dek: iron-bar xylophone

kong thom: 16 inverted bronze bowls hung in a semicircular frame, and played by two small hammers

kong toch: a small gong

skor thom: 2 big drums similar to timpani

sampho: a horizontal drum with two heads

tching: two small alto cymbals for marking the time measure, or sticks of hardwood or bamboo for the same purpose

Comparing this with the Thai Pi-Phat instruments listed in the chapter on Royal Thai Ballet, some minor differences will be noted.

There is no written music; musical modes indicative of emotions, moods, seasons, time of day, etcetera, are handed down by memory from one generation to another; so that Cambodian music, while remaining true to style and conserving its form and character, still has a great deal of flexibility, especially in the hands of highly talented musicians. The Royal Palace at Pnompenh maintains as part of the Royal Ballet 9 musicians, 24 choristers, 2 soloists, and 2 readers. During performances, the readers recite or declaim the story enacted by the ballet. The choristers sing with the instruments, taking up and elaborating the themes recited or declaimed. They also beat the measure. Curiously, most musicians in Cambodia say they are Filipinos. The two palace musicians who kindly gave me melodies from the Royal Ballet music, copied into European notation, were Filipinos.

Dance Performances

Pnompenh, the capital of Cambodia, is built around the Pnom or hill. This hill is crowned by a pale-gray stone stupa where, legend says, a small statue of the Buddha once miraculously appeared after a great flood of the Mekong River. The Pnom is planted with trees, and its slopes are lawns. At the top, adjoining the stupa, is a lovely little Buddhist temple with wind-bells hanging all around the edges of its roofs. A broad stairway leading from the foot of the Pnom up to the temple is lined on both sides with mythological animals to guard the approach to the temple. On the other side of the Pnom is a zoological garden where handsome imperial tigers do not deign to look at miserable humanity, but roar their loneliness to the moon.

The first Cambodian dance performance I saw was one whose presentation was directed by impeccable French taste. It was Princess Say Sang Van's ballet, and was danced at the foot of the Pnom on a platform built for the purpose. The pale-gray stupa in the background high above was lit by floodlights hidden among the trees. The soft Cambodian wind was perfumed with the scent of flowering trees. The dancers, in gold brocade and jeweled costumes lit by spotlights, were entrancing in that natural setting. Their golden headdresses repeated again the form of the stupa in the background, and the stupa itself, under the floodlights, appeared translucent— a faery thing.

The next occasion was during the *Fête des Eaux*, the "Fete of the Waters." This takes place once a year when the great Mekong River (one of the longest rivers in the world, which flows from the Tanglha Range in Eastern Tibet into the South China Sea) pauses for a moment and begins to flow backward. The astronomers know what day and what hour this phenomenon will occur, and as the life of Cambodia is intimately connected with the Mekong, everyone takes part in the traditional celebrations, which last a whole week. The town of Pnompenh is decorated. The King changes his residence from the pink-walled palace to the royal houseboat on the river. In a procession of elephants in elaborate trappings, beflowered motor-cars, and decorated officials, His Majesty is carried on a golden throne on a gold-lacquered platform borne on the shoulders of many servitors. High over the King is carried the traditional golden parasol, symbol of royalty and sanctity since ancient times throughout the East. The sculptured kings of Angkor have identical parasols over their precious heads. The Achaemenidian kings of Persia, 2,500 years ago, sat under such parasols, and they took their customs from Bablyonians, Assyrians, and Egpytians whose kings were also sheltered by parasols. In the palaces of Java today, the sacred texts and the books wherein the dance and music are recorded are carried under parasols even for rehearsals.

For the *Fête des Eaux* Cambodians come from far and near, from every province, to take part in or to witness the celebrations. Fireworks and street processions of amusing and clever paper figures, with lantern processions at night, make the town gay. Within the pink-red crenelated walls of the palace enclosure, in a spacious pavilion beside the famous Silver Pagoda, provincial ballets requested for the festivities dance all day. Anyone may come and watch. As the pavilion is open on three sides, the spectators sit where they wish, or where there is room to sit or stand. The ballets I saw there had excellent and well-costumed star dancers. They danced their very best, for if they pleased some palace talent scout they might be chosen for the King's ballet which would be a great honor, and their families would be well provided for ever after. There appeared to be quite a large membership in the ballets I saw, and in certain scenes representing processions or a trip to another locality, the whole troupe took part following the leading dancers, getting smaller and younger and less adept and less well costumed until the last tiny tots stumblingly brought up the rear, practically in rags, and doing their best not to forget the dance figures.

On the concluding day of the *Fête des Eaux* there is a beautiful regatta on the Mekong. Each canoe, extremely long and slender, is painted a different color. The rowers are dressed in uniforms that contrast harmoniously with the color of their canoe, and the oars are painted all of a color on one side with gold or silver on the other, so that their dipping and flashing in the sun are the more accentuated. All these canoes moving down the river are a uniquely beautiful sight. During the race their speed is amazing: each canoe does its best to win the yearly prize, and honor the village or community from which it comes. During the regatta the King and his guests watch from the royal houseboat where the King lives the whole week of the festival. At the end of the regatta, the winners row alongside the royal houseboat and the King personally bestows the prizes. In the evening after the regatta, there is a display of fireworks on the water; and then, out of the darkness over the river, appears a sight straight from the land of legends: the royal dancers, gleaming in their golden, jeweled costumes, dancing on a floating platform. They drift past the royal barge, past the pavilions on the riverbanks crowded with spectators, and disappear again into the darkness and distance. Only the tinkling, rippling music that accompanied them comes floating back to us. So brief, so lovely, so intangible, the passing of the Royal Ballet, apparently dancing on the water, seemed a mirage—an imagined vision.

During my visit to Angkor, Madame Say Sang Van's troupes came up to dance a series of performances in the evenings on the broad terraces of Angkor Vat, the famed Temple of Angkor. Vat or Wat means "temple," and the modern Buddhist temples in Cambodia and Thailand are called Vat or Wat. With the ruins for background, the ballet was danced on a wide terrace, and visitors sat about on the Naga-serpent balustrades or on the ancient steps. The moon cast its green-blue light over the scene, highlighting the trees of the surrounding forest and the great towers and roofed galleries of Angkor Vat. The dancers were illuminated by electric floodlights, but formerly they danced by flickering torches, which I felt would be more appropriate in that enchanted setting. The electric lights gave a hard, unvarying light.

From time to time the warm jungle wind brought the calls of forest creatures, or the pungent odor of bats from recesses of the ruins. The idea of having a living Cambodian ballet dance in front of the sculptured walls of their ancestors, the Khmers, was an example of the French aesthetic sense. Magnificently impressive it was, and I have met people on the other side of the world who, when Angkor is mentioned, catch their breath and exclaim: "Oh, I saw the Cambodian ballet dance there one night. . . ." But my feeling was that to appreciate fully the *art* of Cambodian dance, it should be seen in a less imposing setting, for the delicate play of fingers, toes, and eyes was overwhelmed by the stupenduous background of Angkor Vat.

It was King Sisowath Monivong's birthday, and my brightest hope was to materialize: I was invited to the palace to see the King's dancers perform that evening. The palace walls and gardens were all charmingly illuminated. The up-turning roofs and spires of all the buildings within the palace enclosure, outlined in small electric lights, looked like so many Christmas trees or a fairy city at night, so fantastic and dainty an effect they made against the dark sky.

The guests for this evening, upon arriving by motor or by *pousse-pousse* (rickshaw drawn by bicycle), were shown by uniformed attendants up a broad staircase to the *Salle de Danse,* the pavilion dedicated to the King's ballet performances. Open on three sides, it had lovely paintings of dancers decorating the wall of the fourth side and covering the ceiling from which hung crystal chandeliers. The *Salle* was a rectangle, and along the two long sides ran daises the full length of the room. In the center of one dais stood a throne-chair for the King with other chairs on both sides for his courtiers and the French Resident. On the other dais, facing the King, the other guests sat in comfortable chairs. The evening I was present, there were only about thirty guests. At the far end of the *Salle* sat the musicians in a group, tuning their instruments. The dancing space was the whole floor between the daises with a red and gold tiang (bed-table) placed at each end.

Presently the King, followed by the French Resident and Madame, his wife, and courtiers and other French and Cambodian officials came in and took their places. The guests all rose and bowed to their host, the King. The musicians then played the Cambodian national anthem and the Marseil-laise. The Marseillaise, played on Cambodian instruments, sounded very well indeed, although more celestial than martial. The King and Cambodian courtiers wore the ceremonial costume: a purple silk sampot draped into trousers, and a tailored coat of white in European cut, with decorations and insignia set with rubies, emeralds, and diamonds on the left breast, or hanging by ribbons from the neck.

When all were seated, the King gave friendly nods to those guests whom he recognized, sitting opposite; then refreshments were passed by servitors: tea, bonbons, and delicious petit fours. The orchestra began to play, and suddenly the floor between us and the King was filled with the most exquisite creatures imaginable. They were aglow with gold and little mirrors that flashed lights; the air was filled with the perfume of champaka flowers hanging from their golden mokots (headdresses) and from the jasmine-flower bracelets on their wrists. The features of their white-painted faces were dainty, and their expressions of expressionlessness were fascinating. I remembered what Princess Say Sang Van had told me one day during a lesson: "Don't smile with your mouth. Smile with your eyes." That was what these royal dancers were doing—smiling with their eyes. How beautiful! The "impersonal" faces were each alive with individuality—with a light that shone from within.

Attendant on the dancers, according to ancient tradition, are two old women. They represent "guardians," and pick up fallen jewels, straighten costumes, and make themselves useful in other ways during the dance. In Java, also, the tradition of two guardians for the court dancers is conserved.

As the music of the roneats rippled and purred or tinkled like fairy bells or cascaded like celestial rivulets, the ballet moved through lovely groupings: ensemble dances, solos, duets, with intervals of speaking gestures performed on the bed-tables to tell the story of the ballet. The postures were perfect in sculptural harmony and rhythmic flow. There was a love scene on one bed-table enacted by a prince and a princess. According to tradition, the "princess," with dainty gestures and little screams, rejected the amorous advances of the "prince." The King was especially delighted with the girl, a real beauty, who played the part of the prince. He watched her, constantly smiling, and many times during the ballet, beckoned to one of the two guardians, who came hurrying across the dance floor, crouching amid the dancers as inconspicuously as possible, to the King, where she knelt before His Majesty with her hands in Anjali. The King then handed her a package of money, indicating the dancer on whom he wished to bestow it. The old woman would place it on a silver tray, and crouching again inconspicuously among the dancers, would kneel before the chosen one, proffering the tray and the present. The dancer, with no sign of recognition other than a lowering of the eyes to rest for a brief second upon the offering, danced straight on. The old attendant then carried the tray and package to the exit door where the dancer would claim it after the ballet. The "princess" received such awards twice; two secondary dancers, once each; but I lost count of the kingly favors to his favorite, the "prince." The ballet lasted about two hours and was by far the most beautiful Cambodian dancing I had seen.

Dance Technique

The technique and exercises of Cambodian and Thai dance are identical, as explained in the chapter on Thai Royal Ballet.

Head: carried erect and level, "nobly," under the heavy tchedah or mokot. Slight inclinations correspond to the body posture or to the emotion expressed at that moment. Dancers playing giants, warriors, and all virile masculine roles carry the head high and arrogantly. Women and "gentle" masculine roles carry the head modestly and introspectively. Comic characters carry the head tilted, and use quick movements or other attitudes suitable to the parts.

Hands: make full use of wrist and finger flexibility. In the straight dance sequences, the hands assume one of two positions: pataka or hamsasya. These have only decorative value in these sequences. In the dramatic interludes, the repertoire of hand-speaking gestures is very great. (See also illustrations for both Thai and Cambodian Dance chapters for a few examples.)

Arms: possess great flexibility. In straight positions, the arm is so intensely straightened that the elbow joint is thrown *in* to give the admired inverted bend to the arm. When the arms are raised, the elbow should never be higher than the shoulder in the feminine roles, and only slightly higher in the vigorous masculine roles. There is an effective movement of the arms achieved by alternately flexing and straightening the elbows, arms being opened to the sides, at shoulder height, the hands in hamsasya position.

Torso: erect except in dramatic moments when its assumes an appropriate expression and inclination.

Knees: deeply flexed for all poses. A posture is often taken on one leg, the arms and hands describing certain movements while the supporting knee alternately flexes and straightens. Another posture is with both knees flexing and straightening slightly, giving a springy effect. There is a remarkable "walk" on the knees, used to approach a high personage. It is the most unusual and rhythmically beautiful manner of progression imaginable. (See under Theatre Conventions.)

Feet: in walking they are placed slightly turned out, with toes lifted. In running the feet are placed normally. In certain dance movements, the ball of the foot lightly taps the floor in a ballet third position, half-toe, alternately in front of and behind the supporting foot. The heel of the supporting foot also alternately rises and falls again to the floor. An *arabesque Siamoise* is preceded by a tap of the foot on the floor, signifying a "takeoff" into the air since a Thai arabesque is a "flying" position. A rapid beating of the feet on the floor signifies excitement, and a thump of the heel denotes anger or decision. Rapid *bourrées* in ballet *plié en seconde* are often used in masculine roles as a mode of progression in scenes portraying battles or excitement.

Manner of sitting: for Anjali, both sexes kneel, sitting on the heels with toes in half-toe position; feminine knees are placed together, masculine knees are spread. In other sitting postures, women sit with both legs to the right side, toes turning up, and hands on the right thigh, palms down. Men sit on one leg with the other knee raised.

Speaking Gestures

In addition to the dance technique, a special and most fascinating characteristic of Cambodian and Thai dance drama is the use of "speaking gestures." There is a large repertoire of these gestures which are conventionalized. I shall describe a few to give a tangible idea of their meanings. The narrative parts of the ballet usually take place when the dancer is seated on the tiang, a wooden platform raised about 18 inches above the floor like a bed or low table, and which I have referred to in the text as a "bed-table."

Anjali: ceremonial salute performed at the beginning and end of the dance. Executed thus: the hands are raised, palms together, fingers slightly spread and bending back, to the forehead, thumbs touching the forehead. The hands are then lowered to the breast with a slight bow and a slight turn of the wrists; then again raised to the forehead with a slight bow.

Musti: clenched fists, means fight, war, battle, quarrel.

Sorrow, weeping: head tilted down, hand raised to eyebrow level and almost touching the brows, palm down.

Caress, love: one person touching another on the chin.

Love: arms crossing on breast slowly and gently.

Confusion, embarrassment: head averted, palm on cheek, fingers bending back.

Listen, or I'll tell you: index finger pointing up.

Entreaty: arms extended, palms up.

"Come here": fingers tapping the floor or bed-table three times.

I, myself, me: index finger and thumb joined in hamsasya, other fingers spread; hand placed palm in at breast.

Calling attention to the gods or to the sun: pointing heavenward and looking in same direction.

A meeting or coming together: bringing hands together, palms down, right hand on top of left.

Distraction or indecision or worry: rubbing behind the ear with side of hand, palm out.

Surprise, joy, pleasure: clapping hands three times.

Anger, impatience: stamp of the foot.

THEATRE CONVENTIONS

Anjali is the reverential salute to high personages, to royalty, or to sacred objects. It is achieved by placing the palms together at forehead height, the fingers spread and turned back so that the gesture suggests a flower or chalice being offered. Anjali at breast is the salute to equals.

A journey is indicated by a *tour-de-scène* in a march-time step.

Approach to a royal personage is performed by a remarkable walk on the knees accomplished thus: in ballet first-position *plié* to the floor. Fall onto the right knee, right hand palm down on the right knee, left hand at left hip in hamsasya. Step forward with left foot, and fall instantly onto the left knee, reversing the hands and bringing the heels together. The head faces the direction of progression continuously. Repeat this "walk" until within an appropriate distance from the royal person.

Combats are executed with weapons and shields striking as the warriors circle each other with a rapid ballet *bourrée en seconde*.

Love scenes are always played sitting on the tiang (table-platform) referred to under "Dance Properties." The Princess always repulses her Prince-Admirer with little gestures of deprecation accompanied by little screams and turnings-away.

Scenery and change of locale exist only in the imagination of the spectators, evoked by the acting of the dancers. The only stage furniture is the tiang referred to above. This is about knee high, and serves as a bed, a platform, a house, a palace, a throne, and so on. Love scenes are always played on it.

Some of the principal characters appearing in Cambodian and Thai ballets are:

MASCULINE
Gods (played with masks)
Kings
Princes
Governors
Officers
King or Prince of yakshas or yeak (giants) played with masks
Yakshas or Yeak (giants)
Kinnara (celestial singer)
Gandharva (celestial musician)
Hanuman (white monkey) with mask
Nillaphat (black monkey) with mask
Sugriva (red monkey) with mask
Bali (green monkey) with mask
Garuda (the eagle) with mask

FEMININE
Goddesses
Queens
Princesses
Governors' wives
Ladies-in-waiting
Kinnari (celestial singer)
Nang-Ma-Tcha (mermaid or River Goddess)

Dance Exercises

Exercise I.

Stand on left foot, right foot one-half toe, fifth position in front of left foot.

Left hand pataka, arm raised at left to shoulder height.

Right hand hamsasya, right arm extended down at right.

Starting from this pose, looking at hamsasya hand continually:

Step on right one-half toe, extending right elbow to right (on count 1).

Step on left heel, bending right elbow (on count 2).

Step on right one-half toe behind left foot, extend right elbow (on count 3).

Step on left heel, bending right elbow (on count 4).

Repeat for 14 counts, stamp right foot, and reverse to left. Continue repeating until perfection is attained.

Exercise II.

Step forward on right foot, raising arms with pataka hands (on count 1). Tap left foot one-half toe behind right foot, with wrist movements so that left hand comes into pataka, palm up; and right hand comes into hamsasya, extended to right side, shoulder height. Look at hamsasya hand (on count 2).

Step forward on left foot, raising arms with pataka hands (on count 3). Tap right foot one-half toe behind left foot with wrist movements so that right hand comes into pataka, palm up at right side; and left hand comes into hamsasya extended to left side, shoulder height. Look left at hamsasya hand (on count 4).

Repeat until perfection is attained.

Exercise III.

Step forward on right foot, raising arms, elbows completely extended with hands in pataka (on count 1); look front; *plié* on right knee, simultaneously lifting left foot in "flying pose," and with turn of left wrist so that left hand comes into pataka, palm up at left side, elbow at shoulder height; right hand comes to pataka, palm facing right, right elbow bent in right angle (90-degree angle) at right side (count "and").

Holding this posture, arms motionless, alternately straighten and flex (*plié*) right knee to the utmost, for 16 counts: 1 and; 2 and; 3 and; 4 and; 5 and; 6 and; 7 and; 8 and; 9 and; 10 and; 11 and; 12 and; 13 and; 14 and; 15 and; 16; stamp on right, reverse to left.

The accent is *always* the upward movement, that is, on the straightened knee.

The upward accent gives lightness, an aerial effect.

Repeat until perfection of posture and equilibrium are achieved.

Exercise IV.

Repeat Exercise III, turning in a circle to the right for 8 counts; reverse to left foot, and turn in a circle to the left for 8 counts. Continue this exercise until perfect equilibrium and control are attained.

Exercise V.

Step forward on right foot, raising arms, elbows extended, hands in pataka (on count 1). Look front.

Plié on right knee, simultaneously lifting left foot into "flying pose," and turning left wrist so that left hand comes into pataka, palm up, at left side, elbow at shoulder height; and right hand comes into hamsasya, palm up, right arm extended backward, right wrist almost touching left heel.

In this pose, alternately straighten and *plié* right knee to the utmost, 16 counts, as in Exercise III. Stamp right foot, and reverse to left. Continue this exercise until perfect equilibrium, ease, and control are attained.

Exercise VI.

Repeat Exercise V, turning in a circle to the right for 8 counts; reverse to left foot, and turn in a circle to the left for 8 counts. Continue this exercise until perfect equilibrium, ease, and control are attained.

Exercise VII.

Step forward on right foot, raising arms, elbows extended, hands pataka. Look forward (on count 1).

Plié on right knee, simultaneously lifting left foot in "flying pose" and turning wrists so that hands come into hamsasya at shoulders, thumbs and index fingers of hamsasya touching shoulders. Straighten right knee, extending arms completely to sides, hands remaining hamsasya (on count 2).

Plié right knee, bringing hamsasya hands in to touch shoulders (count "and"); continue *plié*, facing front, for 16 counts; stamp right foot, and reverse on left foot.

Continue until perfect poise, equilibrium, and control are attained.

Exercise VIII.

Repeat Exercise VII, turning in a circle to the right for 8 counts; reverse to left foot, and turn in a circle to the left for 8 counts.

Continue until perfect equilibrium, control, and poise are attained.

A PRINCESS IN AUDIENCE WITH A KING OF THE YEAKS

(For practice of speaking gestures)

The Princess enters the court of the Yeak King, and salutes him with Anjali. The King greets her with Anjali, and tells her it is a pleasant surprise to see her in his court; what news does she bring?

The Princess replies that she has something to tell him. She has come from her realm to tell him news of a grave nature. Her realm is menaced by a powerful enemy. Her father, the King, is greatly worried, for he cannot resist. There will be war, and many will die. She wishes to avert this, so she has come to entreat the Yeak to lead his army to their aid. The

Yeak listens attentively, then considers his forces, the military strategy, counts his troops; he gives his consent to the Princess. The Princess, who has been waiting tearfully and anxiously for the Yeak's decision, now thanks him with deep gratitude, and leaves his court, returning home joyfully.

Action: The Princess enters in a diagonal across the stage in the manner of progression described under Theatre Conventions: Approach to a royal personage. She stops at a short distance from the Yeak King's throne. From her kneeling position, she salutes the Yeak with Anjali, then sits in the Thai-Cambodian feminine manner described above.

Yeak: seated on his throne (tiang) makes Anjali to Princess; points to her with right hand; makes hamsasya on his breast, then claps his hands three times. Looking at her, he points up.

> *Meaning:* "Greetings to you, O Princess, your presence . . . to me . . . gives great pleasure. . . . What news do you bring?

Princess: sitting before the King, makes hamsasya at her breast with left hand, looking at Yeak, then raises her left hand to point up.

> *Meaning:* "I . . . will tell you, O King."

Hamsasya with left hand at her breast; right arm extends pointing right; left hand, palm out, index finger pointing up, moves side to side in negative sign.

> *Meaning:* "I . . . come from my kingdom . . . to tell you grave news."

Rising onto knees, right hand points with arm fully extended to right.

> *Meaning:* "my kingdom."

Remaining on knees, right hand snaps index finger across face.

> *Meaning:* . . . "is menaced."

Remaining on knees, looking right profile, rubbing left ear with left pataka hand six, seven, eight times.

> *Meaning:* "my father is greatly worried."

Remaining on knees; looking at Yeak, extends arms completely to right and left, hands in musti.

> *Meaning:* "there will be war."

Remaining on knees, brings hands in front of body in hamsasya, turns wrists, hands open to pataka, palms facing audience, fingers down. Head inclined to look down at hands.

> *Meaning:* "many will die."

Sits in Thai-Cambodian feminine manner; looking at Yeak; hamsasya at breast with left hand; left arm opens left, left hand opens to pataka, palm facing audience; shakes hand in negation.

> *Meaning:* "I . . . wish to avert this."

Anjali toward Yeak with pleading look.
Meaning: "so I entreat you to come to our aid."
Sinks into gesture of weeping, leaning on left hand for 16 counts; followed by gesture of anxiety, for 16 counts.

Meanwhile the Yeak King, seated on his tiang throne, has listened attentively. As the Princess weeps, the Yeak thinks deeply with left index finger at his temple (for 8 counts), looking right. Yeak grips chin with right hand, looking left (for 8 counts), left hand at left hip.
Yeak: Left hand open, fingers spread:
Right hand turns little left finger down on left palm (for 2 counts).
Right hand turns third left finger down on left palm (for 2 counts).
Right hand turns middle left finger down on left palm (for 2 counts).
Right hand turns index left finger down on left palm (for 2 counts).
Places right hand on right thigh.
Left index finger opens out (2 counts).
Left middle finger opens out (2 counts).
Left third finger opens out (2 counts).
Left little finger opens out (2 counts).
Meaning: counting the Yeak armies.
Swings left musti fist across face.
Meaning: "I can do it."
Claps hands three times at his left side.
Meaning: "with pleasure."
Points to Princess, and looks intently at her.
Princess: executes a long, slow Anjali on her knees, bowing her head to the
King.
Meaning: "Thank you in deepest gratitude . . . O King."
Yeak: executes Anjali to the Princess.
Princess: turns and exits on reverse diagonal on which she entered, in
identical manner of progression, that is, on her knees.

During this conversation, the music fades out when the voice of the Narrator begins. Only the tching continues, keeping time for the dance gestures and for the narrator's voice. At the end of the conversation, during the Anjali of the Princess, the music fades in softly as the Narrator's voice subsides.

Concluding Thoughts

Love and understanding of the Cambodian classic dance are deeply rooted in the hearts of the people. The dance is inextricably woven into the traditions of the country, with their philosophy, religion, ways of thinking and doing, and therefore must persist. In the past it has flourished more than at present. At one time, the French Colonial Government made laudable efforts to stimulate and encourage the dance and other Cambodian arts such as textile weaving, bronze sculpture, wood carving, and the superb silverwork, all utilizing patterns, designs, and traditions of the great classic period of the Khmer culture. This has been the particular work of George Groslier, Director of the Musée Albert Sarraut in Pnom-penh, and of Mademoiselle Karpeles, Directress of the Bibliothèque Roy-ale, which she was instrumental in founding. Both she and M. Groslier are dance enthusiasts. I have already referred to George Groslier's fine book, *Danseuses Cambogdiennes.* His museum has one section devoted to bronze casting, and nearly all the output is little bronze dancing figures. The silver section makes jewelry in the Khmer tradition, and armlets, bracelets, anklets, belts, and other ornaments such as are worn by the dancers in the sculptures at Angkor and by present-day dancers. Another section of the museum makes dance masks and headdresses (mokots).

Xenia Zarina in a posture of sleep: waking from sleep.

Princess Say Sang Van
with two of her dancers.

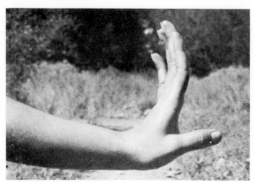

Cambodian dancer's hand in pataka mudra.

The King of Cambodia on a golden throne, under a golden parasol, being carried to his houseboat for the *Fête des Eaux*.

Xenia Zarina demonstrating the full-blown lotus in the dance, Apsaras of Angkor Vat, Angkor Vat, Cambodia.

Star of Princess Say Sang Van's troupe in flying attitude, right hand in hamsasya, left hand pataka.

(*photo by Lindquist*)

Xenia Zarina as Apsaras of Angkor Vat (flying posture).
(*photo by Semo, Mexico*)

Apsaras of Angkor Vat, sculptured on a wall of Angkor Vat.

Xenia Zarina as Apsaras of Angkor Vat in the niche posture. Right hand in hamsasya mudra, left in kapitha mudra. (*Forbes*, *N.Y.*)

Dancers in front of Angkor Vat. Note bending of fingers.

Love scene between Hanuman and Nang-Ma-Tcha. Photo taken in a patio of the Royal Palace, Pnompenh, Cambodia. (*photo by Musée Economique*)

Dance pavilion of the Royal Palace (*photo by Royal Photo, Pnompenh*)

Kinnari "flying" in a patio of the
Royal Palace, Pnompenh, Cambodia.
(*photo by Musée Economique*)

An elopement scene at the ruins of
Angkor Vat (hands in pataka mudra).
(*photo by Siemréap–Angkor*)

Love scene between a prince and a princess (hands in pataka mudra).

(*photo by Siemréap–Angkor*)

Princess Say Sang Van's Ballet. Right hands in pataka,
left hands in hamsasya.

Court Dances of Java

Javanese History

Of the early history of Java and the neighboring East Indian islands, little is known, but from Indian and Chinese records, from the writings of Arab travelers, from Javanese documents, and from archaeological research, it has been possible to reconstruct it broadly.

Before the Christian era there existed in the East Indies a powerful and almost mythical Malayan Empire of which Java was a part, and which carried on a flourishing trade with India, Indo-China, and China. The Malayan Empire also made war on China, and had a sphere of influence over a large part of the Indian Ocean and Southwestern Pacific. The religion of the Empire was an animistic cult, with ancestor- and hero-worship and magico-religious rituals. But when Indian traders came and established colonies, they brought their Indian religious beliefs, and, according to Indian records, Vishnu and Siva cults were established in Java in 78 B.C., with Buddhism following much later and coexisting with the earlier Brahmanism. By the time Central Java became Buddhist, the older Brahmanic cults were preserved in East Java and Bali. In fact, many Sivaistic temple ruins still exist, of which the most notable is the Prambanan group. Laid out along avenues, these fine architectural masses, built of beautifully cut and fitted stone, are enormously imposing.

The Sailendra kings who ruled Central Java in the eighth century (A.D. 750–860) were Buddhists, related to the Sailendra dynasty of Palembang, Sumatra. Under their rule, Indian influence increased. The theatre and dance were greatly enriched by contact with the Hindu theatre whose traditions and gestures had been firmly established and classified in the *Natya Sastra*.

89

During the Sailendra period, the exquisitely conceived Borobodur was built in Central Java. The Borobodur is not a temple, but a monument built to contain a precious relic of the Buddha. It stands on a small hill in a green valley surrounded by mountains. But its appearance was not always thus. Originally the valley was a lake, and the Borobodur appeared as a great stone lotus floating on the waters. Its rising terraces represent rings of petals, and its top platform, which is circular on a square base, is crowned like the center of a water lily by stone "stamens" while in the very center rises, like a pistil, the great stupa that contained the relic. Each stamen has the form of a small stupa, and under its lattice sits a representation of the Buddha. The terraces that form the base of the whole building are quadrangular. They are four in number and are carved with scenes of the Buddha's life. The first terrace shows the meeting and marriage of his royal parents; the second, his birth and youth; the third, his search to relieve suffering humanity of pain, sorrow, and death; the fourth, his enlightenment and attainment to Nirvana. Of particular interest to us are the sculptured panels representing historic dance scenes, such as the daughters of Mara dancing before Lord Buddha to tempt him, and the panels representing court entertainment dances, and the women kneeling and saluting Lord Buddha with Anjali.

In the eleventh century, the celebrated King Airlangga reigned (1019–1049). He was a great patron of the arts, particularly literature and dance dramas. Airlangga's name is connected with one of the oldest and finest pieces of Javanese literature: the *Arjunavivaha*, which is a dance drama beloved of the Javanese from Airlangga's time to the present day. Airlangga's court was famous for its literature and poetry which were presented in dance-drama form during lavish entertainments. Neighboring kings sought to imitate the magnificence of Airlangga's court, thus creating an epoch of artistic development.

The Empire of Majapahit dates from A.D. 1293 to 1525—until the Islamic period—and was a golden age for Java. There was great activity in all the arts, and much literature and poetry were written. Javanese taste and spirit had by this time completely absorbed Indian influences, and produced a true Javanese art in architecture, sculpture, literature, music, and dance.

The violent aggression of Islam put an end to the Golden Age. In the fifteenth and sixteenth centuries, continual disturbances and uprisings against the Moslem invaders led to general decadence in Javanese life and art. The Javanese even sought help from the Portuguese, who had recently arrived on the scene, but were unable to stem the tide, and in about 1525 Islam became established as the official religion. The king, gurus (teachers and wise men), and aristocrats fled to Bali with the remnants of their treasures. About this time European traders, particularly Portuguese and Dutch, came seeking the "wealth of the Indies."

In the eighteenth century, Java experienced a renaissance. Dance and drama again attained perfection at native courts. There were two courts now, for in 1755 the Empire of Mataram was divided, as a compromise, into two states: Surakarta, whose ruler bore the ancient title of Susuhunan, (Axis of the Universe); and Djokjakarta, ruled by a sultan. Two lesser princes were also established as liaison officers between the Dutch traders and the Javanese rulers. These princes bore the titles of *Mangkunegara* of Surakarta, and *Paku Alam* of Djokjakarta. These political divisions and titles were maintained until 1947, but the states still remain the centers and preservers of Javanese culture and tradition.

Elements Forming the Dance

The story of the creation of the dance, told in Java, is a variation of the Hindu legend. All the gods collaborated in the creation of the seven Widadaris (heavenly danseuses). They formed them of precious jewels of finest quality. Then the Widadaris began to dance, and all the gods watched, and when the seven Widadaris had danced three times around the ocean, all the gods had "wismaya" (ecstasy) and were delirious with delight at the beauty, harmony, and order they had wrought.

Another legend, Javanese in origin, tells about Bhatara Guru, the Supreme One, the Great Teacher, who wrought the first gamelan (Javanese musical instrument), then built a holy place, a temple, where the other gods and goddesses danced the very first dance to its sonorous melodies.

Remnants of the venerable belief in the ancient animistic religion, even after centuries of domination by Hinduism, Buddhism and Islam, are still alive today. Dances of that early period were, as is usual, mimetic animistic dances to propitiate or invoke divine forces. They were magico-religious rituals, and although they have completely disappeared in their original form, are distinctly traceable in the masked Topeng dances of today.

During the period of Indian influence, ritual dances, forming part of the Brahmin cult, came with the new religion.

The great Indian dance dramas followed, with their vast repertoire of

significant gestures and mythology, a practically inexhaustible source of
dance dramas. It was during this period that Javanese classic dance took
form and made its greatest development. In the eighth century, during
the Sailendra dynasty, purely court dances were known in Java. Sculptured
scenes on the Borobodur represent such dances which entertained princes
and courtiers.

An appealing aspect of the Javanese dance is the shadow-play theatre,
called Wayang Kulit, or Wayang Klitik, ("Theatre or Drama of Leather")
so named because the figures are cut out of buffalo hide. It is the most
ancient form of the Javanese theatre. It seems this entertainment evolved
as a sort of magico-religious rite from the ancestor and hero cults. The
figures are lined up on opposing sides with the Magic Tree in the center,
on one side representing the powers of Good, on the other, Evil. They are
cut in profile with articulated arms and curiously distorted silhouettes.
Long ago this Wayang Kulit distortion became an element of Javenese art,
and is one of the most charming characteristics of Javanese dance. Wayang
Kulit is still the most popular form of entertainment for the people in
Java today, owing to its inexpensive installation and operation, and the
fact that its plays, characters, and heroes are known and beloved by all.
Motion pictures cannot compete with it.

Another very old form of entertainment incorporating dance technique is the Wayang Golek, the drama of puppets. The puppets, carved in
the round, have articulated arms and necks to which thin sticks are attached
for the purpose of manipulation. While the Wayang Kulit and Wayang
Golek dolls are acting, the voice of the dalang (storyteller) recites the
drama with appropriate intonations and changes of voice, as he operates
the dolls. This convention, as well as the Kulit and Golek movements of
head and arms, has carried over into the Wayang Wong (human theatre)
dance dramas.

Thus we find the Javanese dance composed of these elements: ancient
animistic dances, vestiges of Siva-cult rituals and ancient court dances,
Indian theatre with its Hindu mythology and stylized gestures, Wayang
Kulit (shadow plays), and Wayang Golek (puppet plays).

On these elements, Javanese taste played continually, modifying and
molding them to the national taste and character. Javanese qualities,
blending with Indian, became Indo-Javanese art. Javanese taste and temperament cast away exuberant Indian characteristics which did not accord
with their ideals of modesty and refinement, as, for example: the arms of
feminine dancers in Indian sculpture and dance are raised high above the

head, legs are raised to hip height, while the hip is thrown in an accentuated curve to left or right. In Javanese dance, feminine dancers never raise the elbow above shoulder height, the feet scarcely lose contact with the floor, and hips remain in line with the torso. Even the dance sculptures on the Borobodur, still very Indian in style, are less exuberant and sensual than those on Indian monuments. From this trend developed the purely chaste Javanese dance.

Probably long before the Golden Age of Majapahit, Javanese dance had already become distinctively Javanese in style and feeling, the product of the Javanese spirit that had cultivated it. As it was then, so it has remained until today, the expression of extreme aristocratic refinement, noble grace, modesty, unworldly detachment, and harmonious control which, even when interpreting strong passions, remains calm, self-contained, and distinguished. These are qualities the Javanese reverence and practice in their daily behavior.

Character of the Dance

Havelock Ellis in *The Dance of Life* writes: "The most beautiful dance I have ever seen was the slowest." Javanese court dances, particularly Serimpi and Bedoyo, are undoubtedly the slowest dances in the world. The movements are so controlled that one posture flows imperceptibly into another. The rhythm is that of Nature herself—as clouds drift across a summer sky, constantly changing form; as waves of a tranquil sea swell and subside; as a flower opens and slowly fades; as the sun, moon, planets, and stars rotate in their orbits; as the four seasons succeed one another through eternity. When Javanese dance translates these rhythms through human form, the beauty of monotony and imperceptible change is revealed, conveying a feeling of eternity, and the effect on the spectator is hypnotic.

In 1866, the Comte de Beauvoir, traveling in Java, saw these court dances and wrote: "I became little by little so accustomed to the sweet langour, monotonous and lulling, of the graceful danseuses, that our rapid music and our animated, whirlwind ballets seem the madness of a carnival and not the Art of the Dance."

Javanese dance seeks beauty in all its phases. Even when the qualities of ugliness, arrogance, brutality, and ferocity are represented in a symbolic instead of realistic manner, the spirit of these repulsive qualities is revealed as beauty. Perhaps understanding will be facilitated by the example of motion-picture acting. In the early silent films, actors rolled their eyes, gritted their teeth, and tore their hair to express hatred, vengeance, pain, torture, grief, and allied emotions. Today motion-picture acting has become infinitely more subtle, controlled, suggestive, and, therefore, of greater expressive power. Great acting is the result of spiritual concentration so intense that the whole body and muscular structure react to it and send emotional radiations out to the audience.

Javanese dance has grown from the blending of two elements: Indian and Javanese. In analyzing the dance we find the Indian elements to be: the religious ceremony "Sadjen" performed by dancers before the dance; the ceremonial salute "Sembah" which begins and ends the dance; Ramayana and Mahabharata stories for dance dramas; stylized hand gestures and symbolic actions; head movements and eye movements, and the painting of dancers' faces and bodies with ocher-yellow, the sacred color.

Javanese elements are the ceremonial entrance walks—kapang-kapang and tayoungan; the use of arms, legs, and torsos like Wayang Kulit and Wayang Golek dolls; Javanese historical and legendary subjects for dance dramas; the warrior dances and extremely refined feminine dances; the trancelike execution of dances; and the masked Topeng dances.

Terms frequently used in connection with the Javanese dance are explained in the following list:

Wayang Wong in low Javanese, *Ringit Tyang* in high Javanese, and *Wayang Ourang* in the Malayan language, all mean "human theatre" and are dance dramas using Indian epics or Javanese myths and history as subjects. The most beloved heroes of these plays are Arjuna, Bhima, and Pandji. Wayang Wong is played exclusively by male dancers, boys taking the feminine roles.

Kalana dances represent a warrior preparing to meet his beloved, arranging moustaches, hair, and eyebrows, looking in a mirror represented by the end of his sampour, imagining the pleasure of meeting, dancing his anticipated joy with exuberant vitality. Kalana dances appear in Wayang Wong and in Wayang Topeng plays. They are also presented separately as solo dances.

Kiprah dances are expressions of gaiety, exuberance, or love, and are danced only by princes. Kiprah is the masculine counterpart of the Serimpi dances which are performed only by princesses.

Wayang Topeng are masked dance dramas of primitive Javanese origin. Originally rituals connected with ancient animistic cults, they developed a more complicated form by absorption of Indian theatre conventions and gestures.

Wayang Purwa means "ancient theatre," and applies to the shadow play as well as to human dance dramas.

Dalang is the narrator who recites the narrative of Wayang Wong, Wayang Kulit, or Wayang Golek plays.

Bedoyo is exclusively a feminine court dance, danced by nine girls of the royal palace who are of the royal family or related to it.

Serimpi is a feminine court dance reserved exclusively for royal princesses who dance it only in the presence of the sovereign. Four princesses dance it in pairs, one pair duplicating the other in a very attenuated story of love and jealousy for a historical king.

In Bedoyo and Serimpi dances, very lovely geometrical patterns occur, the girls taking their positions in the floor-pattern with more accuracy than finely drilled soldiers. These dances are a continuation of ancient court dances of the eighth century, and the Javanese even like to say they are the original dances of the seven Widadaris. Certainly they appear dream-like and unworldly enough to be the celestial dances of the seven planets revolving through eternity.

Training for the Dance

Ever since the establishment of dances as part of court life, the Javanese court dancers have been royal princes, princesses, and their cousins who lived within the Kraton (Palace) enclosure. The teachers were also, and necessarily, of the royal family, and the court dances have been kept an exclusively royal entertainment. The only way Javanese outside the court, or foreigners of distinction, could see these royal dances, was to be invited to the Kraton on special occasions when these dances were given. Moreover, it was very difficult to obtain an invitation. It was far from sufficient that one wished to see the dances; one's presence must be desired by the Javanese and recommended (prior to Indonesian independence) by the Dutch authorities. Since the establishment of the Indonesian Republic, the situation has doubtless been modified.

If it was difficult to see these dances, it was impossible for an outsider to study them until 1918 when the late Sultan of Djokjakarta, Hamang-konbouwana VIII, who felt the knowledge of Javanese classic dance should be extended outside court circles, endowed his two brothers, Prince Arya Souryadiningrat and Prince Tedjokoesoemo to establish the Krida Beksa Wirama (School of Dance and Music) to teach children of good families outside the court. Prince (Pangeran) Tedjokoesoemo was the most celebrated dancer in all Java, and the Krida Beksa Wirama is the finest dance school in Java, carrying on the truest and purest tradition. In 1938 it was my good fortune to be accepted as a student in this school.

Gusti Pangeran Tedjokoesoemo's home stands in a walled garden adjoining the Kraton. In front of the house, and connected with it, is a large pavilion—a roof supported on slender columns above a polished floor. This is the Krida Beksa Wirama dance studio. At the far end stand the gamelan instruments, their rich cases of carved wood red-lacquered and decorated with gold leaf, the great bronze gongs hanging in carved and painted racks.

In the garden round about are tall poles, and at the top of each, high above the flowering shrubs, is a birdcage. Every morning the servants hoist the birds up there in the sun and air to give them the illusion of liberty and encourage them to sing. During lessons the soft breeze wafts across the dance pavilion, bringing the fragrance of exotic flowers and the clarion calls of these Javanese birds.

Three nights a week there were men's classes, and three mornings a week, classes for girls. The school in 1938 had over one hundred pupils, and Pangeran Tedjokoesoemo directed and taught the classes personally, assisted by his silver-haired cousin, also a noted court dancer.

The complete course in the dance school is three years, but of course one may go on studying much longer—there is so much to learn. When I first made my application to enter the school, I was refused because I could not remain in Java long enough to complete the course. I still possess that disappointing letter. But my eagerness to study was so great that Mr. J. L. Moens, an exceptional Dutch official and connoisseur of Javanese art, interested the prince in me personally, and when he understood that I was already a dancer, he accepted me, to my great happiness. In addition to class lessons, I took private lessons so that my teachers, Pangeran Tedjokoesoemo and his cousin, were convinced of my sincerity, and gave me special attention during class lessons which helped me to advance even more rapidly.

In contrast to the old method, Pangeran Tedjokoesoemo instituted a finely thought-out plan of teaching which every student follows. The first things learned are the hand positions. The first forty-five minutes of class are devoted to the Sembah (ceremonial salute) and the kapang-kapang (ceremonial entrance walk). A rest period of fifteen minutes follows, sipping tea and talking with the gurus, then another forty-five minutes of dance sequences and scarf play. The scarfs, when worn by women, are called utdet; when worn by men, sampour. The manipulation of the scarf is the most important decorative feature in the Javanese dance. It gives accent, marks the music, gives continuity to the rhythm and line of arm move-ments, makes interesting aerial patterns for the eye, and translates emotional intensity into visible form. Another rest with refreshing tea is followed by the last forty-five minutes devoted to actual dances: Kalana, Kiprah, or heroic dances for men, and Serimpi or Bedoyo dances for girls.

In token of respect and gratitude, each student, as he or she enters the dancing space, salutes the gurus with a Sembah, not the ceremonial Sembah used in the dance, but a less elaborate though similar gesture. And on leaving after the lesson, each pupil again bows to the teachers, bringing his hands, palms together, before his face.

At first I wondered at this leisurely manner of studying the dance, remembering the continuous hours of exhausting ballet lessons and operatic ballet training I had become accustomed to: *barre*-work, ballet lesson, rush down to the stage for orchestra rehearsal, back again upstairs for costume fittings, an hour for lunch, all afternoon practicing dances for tomorrow's opera, an hour for dinner and rest, lying on the dressing-room floor (Oh, how good it was just to lie down!), and the opera performance in the evening. Then the long trip home to the suburbs, perhaps in a snowstorm. But such gyrations would never do in the hot Oriental climate. No, their way is the right way for Java, I soon became aware, as I had already become conscious of their high artistic achievement, devoid of breakneck physical feats and useless demonstrations of physical energy that only serve to emphasize terrestrial limitations. In contrast, Oriental dance enables the dancer to fly through the air, dematerialize, and possess other remarkable powers, because of its evocative nature.

Usually there is no music to accompany the classes, but our guru rapped on a sound box (keprak) with a wooden hammer to mark the time. On certain occasions the classes would be accompanied by the wondrous sonority of the gamelan instruments, played by students of the music-school section of the Krida Beksa Wirama.

It was absorbing to watch the men's class in the evening dancing to the gamelan. The electric lights threw a flickering, torchlight effect over the sixty young men and boys of assorted sizes (some very small but very accurate dancers) all moving in unison, throwing their sampours, turning, posturing, catching the end of the sampour again and fluttering it to indicate emotional intensity, heads executing the patjak-kulu movement, stepping with high, virile, masculine leg movements, turning, dropping on one knee, all exactly synchronized with the ringing melodies of the gamelan and the deep bell tones of the gongs. Or to see the Sunday morning girls' class, thirty descendants of the Widadaris moving in ecstatic trance through geometrical figures, throwing their bright-colored utdets in unison, balancing the almost nonexistent weight of their slender bodies from foot to foot in an undulating sway—then with a sharp gedruk movement of their little feet throwing all their trains to the other side like the lash of serpents' tails, and at the stroke of a gong, flying through the air with their utdets as wings.

But if it was beautiful and evocative to watch, how infinitely more so to take part in—to be a part of! The memory of the serene beauty of those lessons in that open pavilion in the garden—the scented breeze that caressed our arms and fluttered our utdets as we danced in an unworldly ecstasy of spirit—has many times solaced me in the midst of turmoil in other lands which are even farther in spirit than in miles from the Nirvanic, rhythmically coordinated peace of those noble lessons. More than dance lessons, they are lessons in religion, in philosophy, in the realization of the meaning of life and eternity; they are a spiritual education.

Suddenly one understands the legends that the dance is a creation of the gods and a gift to mankind. Suddenly one understands why both spectators and performers approach the dance with a reverential attitude. One realizes that the reason for the power and continuation, all these hundreds of years, of the Javanese dance, and of all Far Eastern dances, lies in this realization which permeates the race.

Costume for the Dance

The classic dance in Java, as in all lands of the East, has preserved in their most elegant and refined forms the ancient traditions not only of customs and manners, but of costumes as well.

The basic masculine costume consists of:

Knee-length pants of silk ikat material.

A kain (length of cloth 1½ yards wide by about 3 yards long) of fine cotton batik in the "Royal Water pattern" design in indigo, brown, and cream stripes. This kain is folded about the waist, over the ikat pants, one end hanging in front, the other behind.

A breast-plaque of gold or silver gilt, hanging from the neck on a chain. Armlets on upper arms, and a kris (Javanese dagger) in the belt at the back.

A headdress that represents an ancient manner of wearing the hair (a large tapering loop from the nape of the neck to the top of the head) combined with a gilded leather crown and soumping (ear ornaments). A sampour (scarf) of silk ikat.

To designate the different roles, there are variations in the headdress. A king's headdress is a high crown with two hanks of hair falling over the shoulders onto the breast. There are other subtle distinctions immediately perceived by Javanese eyes, such as the design on batik, or the way it is folded and draped, which are always associated with certain characters. A quiver of arrows is sometimes worn on the back, or very decorative "wings" of gilded buffalo hide which are worn by those who have the power of flying. In Surakarta, these wings are cut so that the arms pass through ornamental loops of leather, but in Djokjakarta the wings are simply attached to the shoulders.

Ikat material is worth a study for itself alone. Since ancient times it has been imported to Java from India, and has always been highly prized. Its manufacture is most unusual. The threads are dyed in vegetable colors: reds, greens, browns, before weaving, and there is supposed to be something magic about the way the design appears, apparently by itself, during weaving. Ikat is fragile, precious, rare, and therefore is reserved in Java for royalty. The ancient art of ikat-weaving is still practiced in India in Gujerat, near Baroda, where only four or five families still preserve the secret. Ikat is called patola in India.

The classic feminine costume consists of:

A kain of diagonally striped batik of indigo, brown, and cream, worn tightly wound about the legs, starting behind the right hip, once about the body, finishing center front, where the end is carried at the left side in the left hand during the kapang-kapang entrance walk, but during the dance, falls to the floor, and passes between the ankles like a train. The kain is *always* worn so that the batik diagonal stripes descend from the right hip to the left ankle.

A corsage of green, blue, red, brown, or black velvet, embroidered in silver-gilt thread, with a panel in front.

An utdet of any color desired, folded and tied about the waist, and falling to the floor in front. Sometimes the utdet is of ikat.

A gold belt is worn over the utdet to hold it in place.

Armlets on the upper arms, in the form of dragons, of silver gilt or of gilded leather.

A breast-plaque of gold or silver gilt, perhaps set with tiny diamonds.

A headdress representing an ancient manner of wearing the hair, combined with the buffalo-hide gilded crown and the soumping ear ornaments.

This costume is also the traditional bridal costume.

There are numerous small differences between the costumes of Surakarta and Djokjakarta, but it is unnecessary to discuss them in detail. The most notable is a sleeveless jacket of velvet, rather European in cut, trimmed with gold fringes, which is worn by the Djokjakarta danseuses instead of the classic corsage worn in Surakarta.

The Serimpis wear crown headdresses; the Bedoyos wear only ornaments or flowers in the classic knot of their neatly dressed hair. There are variations in the form of the crown headdresses to distinguish the feminine roles.

The restrained color schemes—browns, creams, indigos of the batiks with accents of vermilion, jade green, or turquoise utdets—with discreet touches of gold ornaments, exemplify the exceedingly refined and subtle Javanese taste.

Masks and Makeup

Javanese masks are of great variety. One kind is used for the heroes of the Pandji cycle; another kind is used by strolling players; another, by court dancers; other masks represent animals, and were part of the animistic-cult rituals; and lastly, there are traditional masks used only for celebrating certain public holidays.

The masks used for the classic Wayang Topeng are, of course, the finest. They have interestingly stylized features that show Indian influence. The "refined-type" of mask has white, pale green, pale blue, or pale pink face color, elaborately arched and curled eyebrows and moustaches, the nose fine and pointed, the eyes with gilded eyelids half closed in serene contemplation. The "virile-type" of mask has a red, deep pink, or orange-colored face with bushy eyebrows and bristling moustaches, the nose thick and rounded, the eyes round and bulging. I have in my collection four masks: one virile, one refined, and those of their two servants who are comic characters. These have flour-white faces with knobs for noses, squinting eyes, and no lower jaw, so that when worn, the actor's own lower jaw is disguised as a receding chin, giving an "Andy Gump" profile. The refined and virile masks are held in place by a leather thong which the actor holds between his teeth; his is not a talking role, and the dalang recites his speeches. The two clown masks are held in place by cords around the actors' heads, giving them complete freedom to talk. Their parts call for a great deal of improvisation and many comic effects.

The roles of superhuman beings, mythological creatures, garuda (eagle), and monkeys are always played with masks in both Topeng and Wayang Wong plays.

Sometimes, instead of having painted eyebrows and moustaches, the masks have real hair pasted in place. The actual makeup of Wayang Wong actors also follows these two conventions. In Surakarta the actors paste hair moustaches on their faces. In Djokjakarta, they are carefully painted on, following the traditional elaborate curves for moustaches and eyebrows.

The painting of feminine faces only accentuates the natural features: red on the lips, and black on eyebrows and outlines of the eyes. There is a slight idealization of the eyebrow line. Dancers' bodies are painted ocher-yellow, the sacred color.

Dance Properties

Because Javanese dance action is so highly symbolized, not many dance properties are used. The kris, worn in the belt at the back, should be considered as part of the costume since it is part of the ceremonial dress of princes. Lances are carried by followers of a warrior-hero. Short daggers and shields are used in some combat scenes, bows and arrows in other masculine dances. In feminine roles, the goddess Srikandi often appears wearing a quiver of arrows. Both Bedoyos and Serimpis may carry bows and arrows, or small krises and shields in certain dances.

One astonishing innovation, of which I had heard before I witnessed it at the court of the Susuhunan at Surakarta, is that the dancers suddenly break the celestial serenity of their dances by pulling out and firing pistols. The explosion of several pistols only a few paces away, in the midst of a reverie, is as shocking to artistic taste as it is to the nerves. Everyone hopes this "modernization" will soon be discontinued. Plays representing the time of the East India Company and its misdoings also make use of pistols and sabers.

Music for the Dance

Javanese gamelan music has been called the most truly celestial music possible to imagine on earth. Debussy was charmed by it when he heard a Javanese gamelan at an Exposition in Paris, and went often to listen and take notes. Its influence is noticeable in his compositions.

The role of the gamelan for dance dramas is to accompany, setting

the rhythmic pace for the dance and for the chanted recitations, under-
lining and increasing the emotional interest, creating a perfect unity of
dance, drama, and music.

There are two types of gamelan: gamelan selendro with a five-note
scale, and gamelan pelog with a seven-note scale. The instruments, all percussion except three, are:

gambangs (of wood)	rebab (two-string lute)
bonangs (of brass)	souling (four-note flute)
sarons (bronze bars)	yelempoung (harplike instrument)
kenongs (bronze)	tjblon (drum)
genging (percussion)	kendang (long drum)
gender (percussion instrument	bedong (big drum)
like a xylophone)	gongs of several sizes
panerous (percussion)	keprak (wooden sound box)
kempoul (percussion)	

Every dance is begun by an overture whose melody is played by the
rebab. The basic instrument for setting the tempo is, as usual, the drum.
Gongs mark the musical phrases with their rich, deep tones, and indicate
the beginning and end of dance phrases. And all the while, delicate melodies
played by the other instruments give nuance and expression to the dance
language. There are modes always associated with certain emotions and
actions, for example:

anger, wrath	bhima-kroda
exuberance, exaltation	bindrong
serenity, reverie	ayak-ayakan
combat, war	srebegan
menaces, threats	oulok-oulok

If two contrasting characters appear together, two modes expressing
their types are combined to accompany the scene. There are infinite variations possible in the order and combination of the musical themes, of which
a vast repertoire has been handed down through the centuries.

During the dance dramas, the dalang gives indications to the musicians
as an orchestra leader would. When the task is too complicated, he is
assisted by a *chef-d'orchestre* called lourah gending who gives the dance
tempos. The dalang and lourah gending are seated before the gamelan
players.

For Serimpi and Bedoyo dances, a chorus of women, who sing from time to time, is often added to the gamelan.

When the Javanese dance absorbed Indian attributes, the original Javanese gamelan music also took on Indian musical additions, but possessing greater musical scope than the simpler, more limited Indian instruments, a wonderful music developed. No one who has ever heard a Javanese gamelan played—preferably in Java—can ever forget those rich, sonorous, ringing tones, the delicate nostalgic melodies of the ringing carillon of bronze bars, and those incomparable gongs. What an incalculable loss to Western music not to have Javanese gongs in symphony orchestras!

Presentation of the Dance

The court dances are presented today as they have always been, following the ancient Indian tradition whose instructions were written in Vedic times: in one of the Kraton's reception halls, a large pavilion open on three sides with decorative columns supporting the roof, the sovereign and his immediate family take their places. The guests are disposed to the right and left of the ruler on comfortable seats. In this atmosphere, unaided by any special lighting, scenery, or other effects, the art of the Javanese dance simply and unassumingly unfolds itself.

A Wayang Wong Rehearsal

I had the exceptional privilege of being invited to visit several Wayang Wong rehearsals in the Kraton at Djokjakarta where the princes were preparing a play to be given the following year. The way through the Kraton to the rehearsal pavilion was like approaching a sanctuary; as indeed it was a sanctuary of the dance.

We crossed various courtyards where thick green trees cast dark green shade in the bright morning sunlight, through several gates in white walls where Javanese Kraton guards, dressed in traditional costumes of handsome batik dodots, embroidered jackets, and black velvet Moslem hats, presented arms and inspected our entry permits. At last we arrived at a pavilion with three open sides, its roof supported on slender carved and painted columns, where the rehearsal was in progress on the white marble floor.

The play told of the marriage of Krishna's daughter to Arjuna's son.

A large group of Arjuna's men sat at one side, at a distance; an equal group of "women," played by boys, sat opposite. Both groups then made the ceremonial Sembah to each other, after which they rose. Arjuna's men advanced with the ceremonial walk tayoungan, and the women with kapang-kapang until they met. A long conference ensued in Kawi, the ancient classic Javanese language. The actor speaking stood in a wide second position, left hand on hip, right arm extended forward, hand vertical to the arm in nitteng position. This is the traditional posture assumed by a dancer when he speaks or when he represents that he is speaking during the dalang's recitation. In the present case, the recitation was broken up between the principal actors speaking and the recitation of the dalang. Having arrived at a satisfactory termination of the conference, both groups went out, the men with the ceremonial walk tayoungan, fluttering the ends of their sampours in their left hands and fully extended left arms; their right hands in ngepel, alternating rhythmically from extension at the right side to an upward right angle at the right side, the women with kapang-kapang. All the above techniques are outlined under "Character of the Dance" and "Dance Technique" in this chapter.

A pause—everyone seemed waiting for something. And then it happened: two young palace women appeared walking along a marble corridor which connected the pavilions. One carried on her palms an object wrapped in silk; the other, walking behind, held a golden umbrella over the object. As they advanced smoothly across the white sanded courtyard, I had just time to photograph this rare and beautiful sight. The golden umbrella has, since ancient times throughout the East, been carried over a King or over a sacred object, in this case a book of sacred literature, the dance dramas. Ceremoniously the book was delivered into the hands of the dalang, and the maidens retreated as he unwrapped the exquisite silk from the precious document. Now, with the record at hand, the rehearsal could proceed.

Twenty-four demons entered the scene; then the demon-king and fourteen comic characters entered from the other side, and both groups sat facing each other. The comic characters were composed of albinos, dwarfs, and other deformed creatures who live at court to amuse the sultan. Stools were placed for the demon-king and for his general who headed a group of twenty-four demons. They sat facing each other posed in profile like Wayang Kulit figures, and their followers sat in formation behind them. The two chiefs talked alternately about the demon-king's wedding plans. All the followers, at certain points in the discussion, yelled in unison. They planned to make the town beautiful with flowers, and to bedeck themselves to receive the princess, daughter of Krishna. Suddenly a courier arrived with the news that the princess was already married to Arjuna's son. The demon-king gave a great shout of anger—they must make war on Arjuna! Excitedly they discussed war plans. Another courier arrived and sat respectfully before the demon-king, whom he told in rhythmic chant that the demon army had been defeated in another battle elsewhere. Again the king and general conferred, the followers all yelled approval, and all exited in ceremonial walks.

The scene changed again, this time to Krishna's court. Twenty of Arjuna's followers, led by Bhima, appeared, sat, made Sembah, rose, and advanced with the ceremonial walk toward Krishna, where they sat facing him and his followers. Krishna and Bhima sat on stools placed for them, and their followers sat in formation behind. There was a dialogue between Krishna and Bhima: they were glad the wedding had been successfully accomplished. Krishna spoke on one high note as befits a person of distinction; Bhima spoke in a deep, even tone like a gong, suitable to his role as an invincible warrior. The demon-king and demon-general had both spoken in loud, rough voices befitting their coarse natures. Speaking, dancing, and group action were all rhythmically coordinated.

It was now well after noon, and the rehearsal, which had begun early in the morning, was over for the day.

A Dance Performance

One day I received an invitation to a reception at the Kraton of the Susuhunan of Surakarta, and there was to be a Bedoyo dance. My friends, Mr. and Mrs. Moens, called for me, and together we motored along tree-lined roads in the sunset from Djokjakarta to Surakarta. At the gate of the Kraton, we left the car and proceeded on foot across marble floors and white-sanded courtyards until we arrived at the reception hall.

Here the Javanese and Dutch guests stood about chatting until the Susuhunan arrived with his Queen. The guests then formed into line and the Court Minister announced the names of each in turn to the Susuhunan. Rotund and not very tall, His Majesty greeted each guest, who then passed along, bowing to the Queen and to the other wives and daughters who stood in line at the Susuhunan's left, looking like a line of adorable Wayang Golek dolls in their superb batik kains and embroidered jackets. Their black hair, oiled and knotted in a classic Javanese chignon, was ornamented with stars of diamonds and rubies.

All was ceremonious and orderly. Rhythmically the names were called and rhythmically the bows of greeting succeeded one another. Then Mademoiselle Zarina was called. I stepped forward and bowed, but the Susuhunan stepped backward, shouted querulously, "Sarina?" and looking at me with round eyes like those of a "virile-type" mask, incredulously shook his head. As his voice boomed out "Sarina," everyone stopped talking and turned to look. How I longed for the power to dematerialize! Then everyone smiled, for Sarina is a Javanese girl's name and the Susuhunan was astounded that a foreigner should bear it. I bowed again, and all the little queens and princesses smiled and spoke to me as I passed down the line, for they knew I had come to Java to study their classic dance.

As the last guest was presented, all took seats indicated to right or left of the royal family. Refreshments were passed and presently the gamelan began to play. Then, as though suspended by invisible threads, nine Bedoyos moved softly across the marble floor with that unearthly kapang-kapang walk, to kneel in geometrical formation before their sovereign. In motion-less silence they sat, with downcast eyes. Then, as though awaking from a trance, they slowly lifted their eyes to gaze directly at the Susuhunan. Slowly their delicate hands came into Sembah, their lovely heads moved in patjak-kulu, their hands separated, the right returning to rest beside the right knee, the left extending and coming to rest, palm down, on the floor at the left, heads and eyes following the left hand and gazing at a point fifteen feet away at the left side. Again they sat motionless until a gong stroke set all their heads moving in nolah-noleh which brought their faces back to center. Slowly, slowly rising, they now stood, the right hand took the right end of the utdet in gnpulth at the right hip; the left hand, in nitteng tremulously ran down the edge to the left end of the utdet and threw it gently over the left hand with a turn of the wrist, in the dance figure called ngatok. The left feet, which had been unobtrusively seeking the ends of the kains, now found them, and with a gedruk drew them between the ankles and threw them, like little trains, to the right. All the above movements and positions are covered below, under "Dance Tech-nique."

This is the traditional opening for Bedoyo and Serimpi dances. The dance now began, figure after figure slowly, smoothly executed: hands throwing the utdets now left, now right, now back, now drawing them forward, the small feet flicking the little trains now to the right, now to the left. The Bedoyos revolved to a new geometrical formation. Figure after figure—utdets floating in the air and falling again, heads turning, bodies swaying softly like grasses in a gentle wind while the gamelan's clear carillon melodies rippled against the sustained tones of the great bronze gongs, and from time to time a plaintive chant of the women's chorus joined in. On and on they danced like the movement of stars across the night sky. Now and then one of the two elderly women attendants would hurry, crouching among the dancers, to straighten a tangled train or to pick up an ornament that had dropped. These attendants symbolize ancestral protectors and are always present during the dance performances.

Now each Bedoyo unobtrusively drew from her corsage a large, ungainly pistol, and wearily raised it to aim—but the arm and heavy pistol dropped, and heads turned away as though the effort were too great. Again the movement was repeated, again the arms dropped and the feet carried the slender bodies with drooping heads across the floor in vatikangser (sand blowing in the wind). A third time the movement was repeated, and in the midst of the celestial tranquillity a terrific explosion startled all the guests. The Susuhunan beamed with pleasure. All nine pistols had fired, and the Bedoyos, still floating in interstellar spaces, leaned langorously to the right, disposed of the pistols on the floor, and danced on as the original Widadaris had danced—revolving to new positions, forming new, perfectly spaced geometrical figures, utdets floating and falling, feet balancing slender bodies in gentle undulations until, coming back to the original pattern, they sank slowly to kneel again before the Susuhunan and give the final Sembah. For the last time they rose, and with the kapang-kapang walk, disappeared as they had come—silently floating into obscurity.

The dance was over, and one breathed for the first time in forty-five minutes—except for when the pistols went off! The hypnotic spell faded and one became conscious of the world again and of the servants offering tea and trays of alluring Javanese sweetments.

Dance Technique

Gesture is a definite element for determining the degree of civilization of a people. Ancient, highly evolved cultures practice fine and aristocratic gestures, even after the height of political power has long since waned. Ruder people have coarser, more brusque, gestures and manners. While Javanese court dance technique is the essence of aristocratic movement, it is not complicated or involved. It has no extensive repertoire of astonishing movements. Its keynote is simplicity, nobility of bearing, with subtle line and movement. In this it reflects perfectly the national taste.

There are two styles of classic dance: masculine and feminine. The masculine again divides into two parts, the virile type, warriors and villains (the invincible Bhima is the popular hero of this type), and the gentle type, refined, poetic characters, of which Arjuna is the greatly beloved hero. Although male dancers have a wider repertoire of movements, used only by them and never by women, both sexes use the same basic technique as described and listed at the end of this chapter.

The masculine virile type executes postures and movements with widely placed feet and in an extremely vigorous and dynamic, even brusque, manner, according to the character enacted. The sudden leaps and rapid *bourrées* add excitement to combat scenes. The masculine refined type places the feet less widely; and movements, while manly, are executed with elegance and nobility rather than with vigor.

The feminine style keeps always in mind the feminine qualities of modesty, gentleness, beauty, and grace. It is danced with the feet and thighs close together. No leaps break its serenity and elegance. The feminine style is considered more difficult and subtle than the masculine. Above all in fineness and delicacy are the Serimpi and Bedoyo dances.

All the positions and movements, both masculine and feminine, are executed in the style of Wayang Kulit and Wayang Golek figures, that is, two-dimensional poses, clearly marked angles of wrists and elbows, mobile necks and arms, motionless torsos—doll-like, unreal, yet with a continuous, uninterrupted flow of movement from one part of the body to another. Head, eyes, extremities of toes and fingers, are all linked in rhythmic continuity. The movements are performed in such a way that the spectator has the impression that the dancer is animated by an external power. This impression is further enhanced by the trancelike expression on the dancer's face. Or does the spectator have this impression because it is really a fact that the dancers are moved by a force not their own? As a performer of Javanese dance, I must state that the dancer does become possessed by some unnameable power. The utter calm of the Serimpi and Bedoyo dances— the slow closing and opening of the eyes, the patjak-kulu of the head and neck, the langorous lifting and lowering of the arms, the soft transfer of weight from one foot to another—draws one's being irresistibly into a strange psychic state that leaves one refreshed, rested, and indescribably happy. All worries and annoyances vanish; many things lose their importance, or matter no longer. It is medicine for the soul and body, the nearest approach to the nirvanic state that I know of on earth.

SEMBAH (SALUTATION)

Masculine style: sitting on the floor, legs crossed right over left. Raise hands, palms pressed together, before the face, elbows open so that forearms make a straight line parallel to the shoulders. Thumbs touch tip of nose, eyes look straight forward, head executes patjak-kulu.

Surakarta style: fingers point straight up.

Djokjakarta style: fingers point at 45-degree angle with little finger separate from others.

Feminine style: sitting on the floor, legs crossed right over left. Soles of feet full on floor, knees drawn up; hands crossed, left holding thumb of right, resting on top of knees. From this position, raise hands slowly, palms pressed together so that forearms are nearly perpendicular. Thumbs touch tip of nose, eyes look straight forward, head executes patjak-kulu during which movement eyes close and open twice.

Surakarta style: fingers point straight up.

Djokjakarta style: fingers point at 45-degree angle with little finger separate from others.

HAND POSITIONS

Ngrudji: palm facing out, fingers vertical and straight, thumb in line with forefinger, against the palm. Like Indian mudra pataka.

Nitteng: middle finger and thumb joined in a circle. The other fingers curve naturally.

Ngempurit: thumb and forefinger joined against the palm, tip of little finger on joint of fourth finger. Third and fourth fingers curve toward palm.

Gnpulth (Ngepel): meaning a "fist": fingers closed against palm. Little finger tip on joint of fourth finger. Thumb set out at side of palm.

HEAD MOVEMENTS

Patjak-kulu: facing front, the performer executes a figure eight several times with the aid of neck muscles. This movement marks the end of dance phrases.

Nolah-noleh: the head turns from center to profile with a slight lifting, pauses, turns to the other profile with a slight lifting, pauses, turns back to center with a slight figure eight movement.

ARM POSITIONS

Flexed at elbow, upper arm vertical, forearm horizontal and extending forward. Hand vertical to wrist. A slight space between elbow and body as in statues of Hindu gods and statues of the Buddha.

Fully extended straight out from the shoulder, to side or front.

Fully extended down at 45-degree angle.

Elbow flexed to side with hand placed on thigh or hip.

Elbow flexed to side when hand is at shoulder or waist.

TORSO POSITION: always immobile and erect with straight spine.

FOOT MOVEMENTS

Nidath: transfer weight from one one-half-toe to other one-half-toe.

Gnutot: relevé and *plié* on one one-half-toe, the other foot full on the floor. *Plié* until the heal touches the floor, rise to one-half-toe, *plié* again, repeating several times with a smooth, springy action accomplished by slight knee flexations.

Jinjit: relevé.

Gedruk: scoop the train of the kain back with the heel, tap the floor with one-half-toe just behind the supporting foot.

EYE MOVEMENTS: these are of the utmost importance in the expression of the dance; but from the half-closed mata kelipan eyes to the fierce glances and introspective gazes, they are impossible to describe adequately and must be learned from a teacher to be performed correctly.

MANNER OF SITTING

Masculine style: sitting on the floor, legs crossed right over left. Used during Sembah and some other gestures.

Sitting on left heel, right foot full on floor, knees widely separated. Right arm rests on right knee (raised). Left hand on left hip, elbow out at left side. Head looking left or right. Torso erect. A very regal posture:

Feminine style: sitting on floor, knees raised and about 5 inches apart. Ankles crossed right over left, soles of feet full on floor and drawn as closely as possible. Torso erect. Used during Sembah at beginning and end of dance.

Sitting on heels, right knee raised so that right thigh is parallel to floor and touching left thigh. Torso erect. Used during ngla-yang position (ga-jax-ngo-ling). An extremely beautiful posture followed by one of the loveliest movements in Javanese dance.

Manner of Walking

Kapang-kapang: ceremonial entrance walk. Extremely slow and trancelike, as though the executant were floating just above floor. Used only by women. Must be learned from a teacher.

Nyamber: a walk signifying "flying"; performed by walking on very high one-half-toes.

Vatikangser: "sand blowing in the wind"; a sideways progression done by a very smooth shuffling of the feet that illustrates perfectly "sand blowing in the wind."

Tayoungan: ceremonial entrance walk. Used only by men. Step, raise opposite knee to hip height, foot horizontal but with toes raised vertically. Slowly straighten raised leg from the knee to form a horizontal line at hip level, with instep "pointed" but toes raised. Step on the raised foot, and repeat whole sequence. Head and glance follow direction of raised leg. This walk gives very large, open steps, and is an imposing manner of walking. It is done in 4/4 rhythm, counted thus: step and raise knee; count 1; straighten raised leg; count 2-3-4.

Rapid bourrée: executed in ballet *seconde.* Used only by male dancers.

Utdet and Sampour Movements

Ngarakum pangil: take utdet or sampour in gnpulth (fist) hand.

Ngatok: take utdet or sampour in nitteng hand and flip over hand.

Kipat: with turn of wrist, throw utdet or sampour off hand, out of ngatok.

Neblah: flip utdet or sampour up behind with palm of ngrudji hand.

Seblah: hold utdet or sampour in nitteng, and with the first finger, throw utdet or sampour back, meanwhile retaining it in nitteng.

Ngumbat: take utdet or sampour in nitteng fingers.

Nzimpet: take utdet in nitteng and lift wrist to shoulder height.

Sampia: with left palm throw utdet over right shoulder, or vice versa.

Ridong: left end of sampour held in extended left hand, stretched taut. Fourth and little fingers beat sampour to give it a vibratory movement. Used by male dancers *only.*

The utdet and sampour are often used to represent a mirror by holding the left end in the left hand, and "arranging" the eyebrows, hair, moustache, et cetera, with the right hand, meanwhile looking intently into the "mirror."

Combat Steps

Warriors approach each other in rapid *bourrées à la seconde*. Retreat
with the same *bourrée* movement. Repeat several times.
Warriors grasp each other by placing hands on upper arms, and walk
thus in a small circle with large steps, watching each other fixedly. They
break and kneel facing each other in pose described under: Manner of
Sitting, Masculine Style, Sitting on left heel.
Warriors circle each other by walking on half-toes as though "flying,"
and watching each other narrowly.
Great leaps in the air, sometimes with a half-turn, sometimes finishing on
one knee, striking each other's shields with swords.
Falling on one knee and leaning over indicates being wounded.

Speaking Position: Whether the actor-dancer speaks himself, or whether
the dalang speaks for him, he assumes this posture:

Feet placed in a wide ballet second position.
Left hand in gnpulth on the left hip, elbow at left side.
Right arm fully extended forward, right hand in nitteng.
Eyes looking straight forward.

1. Sembah (salutation).
Surakarta style (feminine).

2. Sembah (salutation).
Djokjakarta style (feminine).

3. Sembah (salutation).
Surakarta style (masculine).

4. Sembah (salutation).
Djokjakarta style (masculine).

5. Ngrudji
(similar to Indian pataka).

6. Nitteng.

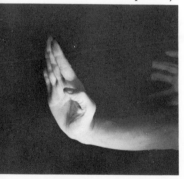

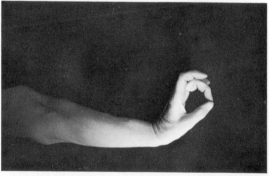

7. Ngempurit
(similar to Indian kapitha).

8. Ngepel
(similar to Indian musti).

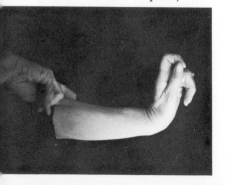

9. Kapang-kapang walk (first movement).

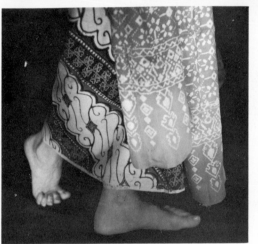

10. Kapang-kapang walk (second movement).

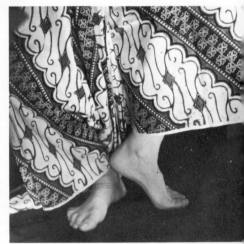

11. Nidath. Transfer of weight from one one-half toe to the other one-half toe.

12. Nidath. Transfer of weight from one one-half toe to the other one-half toe.

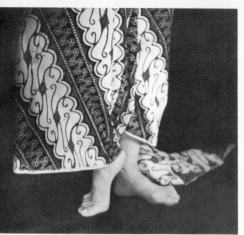

13. Jinjit with right foot.

14. Jinjit with left foot.

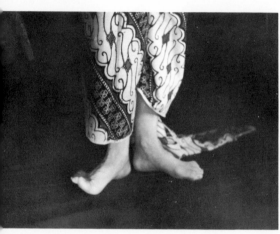

15. Position for swaying from right to left, repeated several times.

16. Gedruk.

17. Nyamber (flying movement).

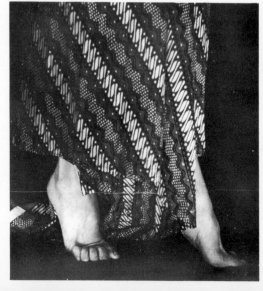

Dance Exercises

Apart from the techniques listed above, we were given no other dance exercises. We practiced the four hand positions, the two head movements, the five foot movements, the eye movements, the manner of sitting, the three manners of walking (feminine)—kapang-kapang, nyamber, and vatikangser—and the utdet and sampour movements until we were at ease in them. We did this voluntarily, in rest periods, not at the instigation of our guru, so that under his tutelage our dance movements would be more correct in the Bedoyo and Serimpi.

Concluding Thoughts

In this chapter I have dealt exclusively with the court dances since they represent the finest and purest tradition in Java, and I have tried to make it clear that they are an exclusively royal court art. Readers may well ask, then, what this art means to the rest of the population, 65 million people, and how can this be a national expression?

Art in Asia has grown from the people as a social expression to fill a social need. It springs from the inner spirit, from emotions and ideals of the race. Racial art forms its people's characters as it was formed by them in the past, the unending circle. It gives intellectual and aesthetic unity. Most especially is this true of the dance and drama, for these arts deal with human affairs, and the material for their expression is not stone, or paper and ink, or paint, but living human beings.

Classic dances and drama conserve traditional customs, costumes, and manners in their most elegant and ideal forms. Javanese national characteristics of self-control, reserve, refinement, ceremonious conduct, dignity, and grace of gesture are ideally portrayed in the dance, even as the national taste is reflected in the subdued dance costumes.

The plays or dance dramas are verse dramas of philosophical and sociological content, representing ideal and noble persons performing heroic acts as models for society. The plays are the classic literature of the race, and are familiar to all, high and low alike. As such, they are a great unifying element, for they express the racial traditions and morality.

While this art of the dance drama in its finest form is conserved at the courts, the common people have the same plays, the same poetic dramas, the same heroes and literature, in Wayang Kulit and Wayang Golek, which can be seen somewhere almost every night. I saw, one afternoon, a Wayang

Kulit being set up in the porch of a Chinese temple in Surakarta, and I saw another one evening in the garden of a humble house. Everyone from the neighborhood had assembled to enjoy it, bringing with them their babies, dogs, and food. While the babies lay sleeping on the ground, the others had picnics, for the play lasted until dawn. It is the custom for the Javanese to engage a Wayang Kulit or Wayang Golek troupe to celebrate some family event, and to invite all their friends to enjoy it.

The people have Wayang Wong and Wayang Topeng, too, in the form of traveling troupes of actors who perform the same dance dramas in a style similar to that practiced in the royal kratons, although of course much inferior in technique and beauty. Instead of speaking in classic Kawi, the popular actors speak everyday Javanese, that is, "low" Javanese, or Malay.

Being the literature, poetry, and ethics of the race, the dance dramas are also educational. Instead of studying literature in school, young Javanese learn it by seeing it enacted with the glamour of costumes, manners, and emotional force of the theatre. Literature, poetry, history, and ethics, instead of being faraway things printed in books, are to the Javanese living events in which people like themselves took part. And the spectators, laughing, weeping, rejoicing, fearing, experiencing the whole gamut of human emotions together, unconsciously create among themselves a great social unity. Knowing, too, that after all it is a play they are witnessing, they develop unconsciously a philosophical acceptance of the Play of Life.

The message and effect of the spoken word are apparent, but foreign minds have to concentrate to perceive the message that the pure dance sequences conveys. In transmitting thoughts, gesture and movement are so much more subtle and rapid than words that minds and eyes become aware of thoughts without realizing how they received them. Gesture and movement, moreover, give nuances of meaning of which words are incapable. And how much more noble and beautiful an expressive medium than words are gesture and movement! In dance sequences the spectators recognize their racial way of moving and resting, posing and gesticulating —an intangible something that belongs to them alone. Prince Arya Souryadiningrat of Djokjakarta called the dance "plastic literature," but it is even more. In the dance surges the very essence of race-spirit.

Regarding the religious ceremony Sadjen which is performed before the dance begins, Th.-B. van Lelyveld in his excellent book on Javanese dance states that incense is burned "out of respectful fear." I fail to understand why Europeans so often think other peoples approach their gods

with "fear"! I have never observed the slightest trace of "respectful fear"
in these ceremonies in any land of the Far East. Rather, I have seen venera-
tion, love, and gratitude for godly protection and benediction. The Divinity
is approached as the Great Friend.

So many people have said, "Oh, yes, Javanese dance—I saw a Javanese
dance in the film *Mata Hari*," that I must say a few words on the subject.
I saw the film, too, and nothing more un-Javanese could be imagined.
The costume was a banal, sparkly, musical-review costume; the dance,
meaningless arm-wavings and unchaste extensions of the legs, snaked
around a hideous plaster nightmare which some Hollywood property man
must have thought looked like what the filmgoing public expects a
Javanese temple idol to look like. The dance was represented as a "Javanese
temple dance." As previously stated, Java has been Moslem since 1525,
more than four hundred years. Previous to that it was Buddhist. Neither
Islam nor Buddhism has any "temple dances." The Brahmanic temples
which *did* have dances as part of the cult, have been deserted ruins for
hundreds of years in Java. The Javanese are horrified and indignant to
have the impression spread that the Mata Hari film dance is representative
of Javanese dance art.

A unique event in Javanese dance history occurred in Holland during
the commemoration ceremonies of the fortieth year of the reign of Queen
Wilhelmina in nineteen hundred thirty-eight. One of the Javanese princesses was in school in Holland, and one of Java's contributions to the festivities was the Bedoyo danced by the Princess Sity Noerail before Queen
Wilhelmina and her court. In faraway Java the gamelan played the accompanying music, which was transmitted by radio from the kraton in
Surakarta to the palace in Holland, while in Surakarta the other eight princesses danced the Bedoto before the Javanese sovereign, leaving vacant the
space occupied by their sister in Holland.

One day during a private lesson, my guru was correcting my posture
and arm position. Suddenly I understood and exclaimed in Malay: "Oh,
like Buddha?" for the posture was identical to that of the Buddha giving
the law. My teacher looked at me, a light came into his eyes, he smiled,
and placing his hand on his heart, said, "Yes, Buddhist." Although Java is
officially Moslem, Buddha's gentle teaching still dwells in Javanese hearts.

Indonesia has obtained her freedom, and the Indonesian Republic is
established, but even when it was still firmly a Dutch colony with no
promise of liberation, many signs pointed to a new day. In Java the desire
for freedom and independence, to be Javanese again, was manifesting itself

in many ways, but the way that concerns this book was the intensified interest in the national arts. The establishment of the Krida Beksa Wirama is an important example, coming as it did from the initiative of a Javanese ruler. The organization of numerous societies of young Javanese who gave performances of Wayang Wong with girl members playing feminine roles instead of boys as in the old tradition; the establishment of other groups, who made every effort to stimulate and encourage art as the best way of resuscitating a national consciousness, are proofs that the arts, the dance, and drama are synthesized manifestations of true nationalism.

Two princes above, servants below. Round-eyed servant belongs to round-eyed prince and slant-eyed servant belongs to slant-eyed prince.

Pangeran (Prince) Tedjokoesoemo.

Borobodur bas-relief showing dance scene before the Buddha.

Reverence to the Buddha, Borobodur, Java.

Wayang Kulit, the shadow play. View behind the screen showing marionettes, the sacred tree, and the dalang (narrator-operator).

The Borobodur, Java.

Prince Tedjokoesoemo with gongs in the dance pavilion, Djokjakarta, Java.

Classmates of Xenia Zarina at Prince Tedjokoesoemo's dance school demonstrating the utdet (scarf) movements: left hand, ngatok; right hand, neblah.

In movements from Serimpi, Javanese princesses Retno and Rennie, author's classmates in Prince Tedjokoesoemo's dance school. (*photos by Hwa Sin, Toegoe, Java*)

Two princesses bring the sacred dance texts, wrapped in silk, across a courtyard in the Kraton (Royal Palace) at Djokjakarta, Java.

Javanese prince executing the Sembah after rehearsal in the Kraton, Djokjakarta, Java.

Princes executing the tayoungan (ceremonial walk) during rehearsal of a Wayang Wong in the Kraton at Djokjakarta, Java.

Princes rehearsing a Wayang Wong in the Kraton, Djokjakarta, Java. Note the sitting posture.

Princes rehearsing a Wayang Wong in the Kraton,
Djokjakarta, Java.

Princes leaving the Wayang Wong rehearsal in the Kraton, Djokjakarta, Java.

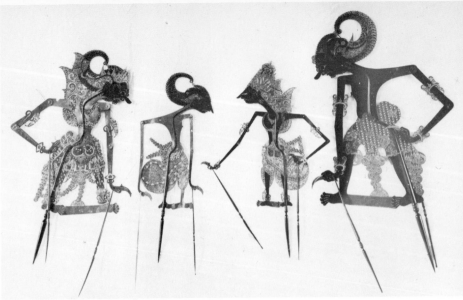

Javanese Wayang Kulit figures cut out of buffalo hide, with horn sticks to manipulate them.

Xenia Zarina in Serimpi, Javanese court dance. Right hand holds utdet in nitteng. Left hand holds utdet in nitteng, preparing for seblah movement. (*photo by Studio Iris, Paris*)

Barong keket (mask).

Xenia Zarina in Serimpi, Javanese court dance. Left hand holds utdet in ngatok. Right hand prepares for seblah. (*photo by Studio Iris, Paris*)

Dances of Bali

Balinese History

ALL THE EVOCATIVE THINGS that have been said and written about the island of Bali can scarcely create, in the mind of a reader who has never been there, a clear vision of the utterly bewitching place that it is. I say bewitching intentionally for there is plenty of magic in the air. Enchantments, spirits, and sorcery are everywhere, and those who visit Bali are possessed by the spirit of Bali ever after.

We do not know much of Bali's early days, but Javanese records from the tenth century onward show that Java and Bali were in close cultural contact. Indian culture came to Bali through Java, and, blending with Bali's native customs and practices, formed what is now known as Indian-Balinese culture. About 1525 when the great Javanese Empire of Majapahit fell before Islam, Javanese royalty, aristocracy, and gurus took refuge in Bali and also assumed political control. Javanese princes became Balinese overlords, and Indo-Javanese culture enriched Balinese life. The Islamic period in Java seems hardly to have affected Balinese life and customs beyond a little trade and a few new subjects for dance dramas.

The Dutch conquest of the East Indies reached Bali also, though late, for in 1906 the Balinese made a last heroic and tragic demonstration against Dutch cannons and warships. In his *Island of Bali,* Miguel Covarrubias describes poignantly how the Balinese dressed themselves ceremonially in gold brocades and flower garlands; then, in a great procession they marched, men, women, and children, old and young, into the sea toward the battleships, singing, until all were drowned.

But, since they conquered Bali, the Dutch officials have really preserved it for the Balinese. Except for a comfortable hotel in Denpasar, the capital in the south, another in Boeleleng, the seaport in the north, for tourists, and a few rattletrap motorcars and bicycles, European civilization has made no impression on Bali. It remains a refuge for souls sick of machinery, industrialization, politics, gasoline, radio, television, and jazz.

The religion of Bali is a mixture of Hindu Brahmanism with Balinese animistic beliefs, and from my observations, I should say the latter certainly predominate. Brahmanism contributed the names of Hindu deities, Ramayana and Mahabharata epics, certain religious forms and ceremonies, and motifs for sculpture, painting, and decoration. The Balinese seem filled with a natural religious attitude, a joyous acceptance of all the good and beautiful things that the Great Source bestowed so generously upon their island. They demonstrate their gratitude by innumerable ceremonies, elaborate processions, painstakingly prepared offerings and rituals, by plays and dances that are also offerings to the gods. Then there are many evil spirits—leyaks—waiting opportunities to manifest their wickedness. To guard against and propitiate these forces, magic rituals have been found an effective, indeed, perhaps the only, way to deal with them. The Balinese, however, never seem to take anything too seriously. They poke fun at sacred things as well as at fearsome ones in their festivities and dance dramas. The clown roles are the usual vehicle for mocking the unseen forces. The audience rocks in glee and inwardly shudders while the clown prances gingerly like someone who has accidentally touched an electric current, amazed at his own risky daring, but gratified by the audience's approval, which incites him to still greater hazards. This genial attitude toward life is what makes Bali and its people so delightful. It may be the reason why solemn missionaries have had so little success in converting the Balinese.

Color of Bali

The "color" of Bali is nearly impossible to describe—the physical color and the spiritual color. One must see it and breathe it and let it impregnate one's being to comprehend it: the blue transparency of the air, sea, and sky; the infinite tones of green in the vegetation; the ranges of color in the clothing of the people, in the pyramids of flowers, fruits, and paper decorations moving in processions along the roads to some gray or brown stone temple nestling in the deep shade of a sacred waringen (banyan) tree; the background of blue, green, lavender, or purple mountains; the colorfulness of all their activities from a group of girls rhythmically pounding rice in shafts of sunlight in a courtyard, or groups of children swinging in the aerial roots of a huge waringen tree, to the most elaborate gold-bedecked ritual. The light and shade of sun, moon, and torches play over these scenes, giving them ever-changing nuances. And there is also the spiritual color of the whole place: thoughts, beliefs, and actions leave vibrations in the atmosphere everywhere in the world, but they seem more intense in Bali.

Early one morning I came to Bali from Java, not as tourists come on big world-cruise ships to the northern port of Boeleleng, but in a little boat across the narrow channel that separates Java and Bali. We landed at Gilimanoeck, a point of land with a few trees. Not a building or a person was to be seen, but over in a clump of trees, a motor bus stood waiting for the boat passengers. My pianist and I followed the others, took seats, and were soon snorting along a pretty road that followed the coast. The weather was like that of a perfect day in May, and we were at last realizing our dream of seeing Bali. Work, study, and fun lay ahead. We could not have been happier.

Suddenly we arrived at a small village, Negara, and were rudely dumped off the bus, bag and baggage. We could not understand a word or ask any questions. No one spoke English, French, Spanish, Russian, or Polish. Our Malay vocabulary was too meager, and the few high Javanese dance terms I had learned had no application to this situation. Moreover, the bus was in a hurry. All we could say was "Denpasar," the name of the southern capital of Bali for which we were headed. We understood from brusque gestures that we were to wait where we were. The bus men did not have time to be cordial. Bus drivers the world over are pressed for time, it seems. We had not the vaguest idea how long we were to wait, or what we were to wait for. It must have been nearly noon, the sun was hot, and we were thirsty and famished. We stood miserably in the dusty road amid our bags. When the dust of the bus's departure settled, we saw a little food booth with the inevitable Chinese cook-owner. (If there are 760,000,000 Chinese in China, there must be an equal number outside. Chinese shops and merchants are to be found on the smallest islands, and such cities as Singapore and Bangkok are practically Chinese cities, the Chinese population being the vast majority.) We ordered something to eat, and while it was being prepared we explored our first Balinese temple which stood nearby: carved gray stone walls surrounding open courts with ornamental open or "split" gateways standing at the top of short flights of stone steps which descend again into the next courtyard. The sculptured walls have niches for offerings, and great waringen trees, the sacred trees, shade the whole place. This is the classic plan of all Balinese temples.

We returned to the Chinese food booth and had barely finished eating when a bus appeared in a cloud of dust. We were grabbed up, put aboard, and buzzed off along the road which presently skirted the sea again. If we had felt happy in the morning, we were in ecstasy now. The scenery became more beautiful with every mile, natives in colorful garments appeared on the road, the bus stopped to take some on as passengers, at other times the driver was given loads of coconuts or bananas, or bouquets of chickens with word-of-mouth instructions as to where to deposit them. Once we stopped for a long time while the driver and an old woman had it out about the cost of transportation for her heap of coconuts. Other villagers gathered around, and all the passengers (who by now filled every inch of space in the bus) joined in the argument with helpful or amusing comments. Finally it was settled and we drove off, our bus groaning and sagging with its load of people, babies, bananas, coconuts, squawking chickens, and even a squealing pig in a basket. Presently, on the open road, we stopped. My pianist and I could see nothing to distinguish this place as a stop, but the driver did. He and his assistant got down, went to the side of the road, placed two or three stones, burned some incense, and with lovely ritual hand gestures, offered flowers, and seemed to be praying. This ceremony took considerable time, but everyone in the bus sat quietly and waited—not even watching!

As we turned inland, villages became more frequent. Rich brown adobe walls thatched with palm leaves were interrupted by gates through which we could glimpse collections of houses, also with brown adobe or cane walls and thick thatches of palm leaves. These were village compounds. The trees became thick and their shade deep over village and road. Even at noon the shade is heavy and dark, but by now it was sunset. Forms and colors were effaced by the dusk, lit only here and there by a level shaft of light from the setting sun penetrating a grove of trees. At last, in complete darkness, we arrived at Denpasar and found comfortable rooms, food, and welcome bath at the big Dutch Hotel.

Next morning, the sunlight, filtered by the branches and aerial roots of the holy waringen tree in the forecourt of the big temple across the street from the hotel, splashed the sculptured gray stone walls with golden flecks. From nearby came sounds of ravishing music. A kebiyar gamelan, the full Balinese "symphony orchestra," was rehearsing. Men, old and young, and small boys sat on the ground dressed in kains and sarongs, playing bronze instruments with mallets. Between their knees, some men held three-, four-, and five-year-old babies, their tiny hands clutching the mallets within the grown men's hands. Thus Balinese fathers teach their children while rehearsing themselves. I stood and listened a long time. The quality of the tones, rich and ringing, the infinite variations of melody, rhythm, and intensity—pianissimo, fortissimo, crescendo, accelerando, abrupt stops, changes of accent in the same phrase as it is repeated over and over at varying speeds and intensities—are all improvised and remembered from generation to generation, each conserving, evolving, and adding to the basic structure.

The shops of Denpasar held many fascinations for me, especially those three or four that dealt in dance costumes and headdresses. There is a small but excellent museum whose intelligent and kindly attendant made friends with me and was invaluable in helping me find among the shops the very best Balinese costumes, or in getting certain parts specially made for me in the best Balinese taste. There was also a Dutch government-run pawnshop where I bought some handsome old batik kains. My museum friend took me to see how Balinese silk brocade with metal threads is woven. In the courtyard of a private house, a girl sat at a loom weaving the delicate threads into rich design of many colors. I watched for more than half an hour, but only a half inch of progress was made, so fine the threads and so complicated the shifting of the shuttles for the design. Another day my friend took me to see an old man who does gold-leaf work on silk, technically known as prada work, for dance costumes and ceremonial garments for Balinese rulers, their wives and children. At a table in a porch he sat painting on a stretched silk piece with a glue made from a native tree sap. Onto the design painted freehand in glue, he then placed squares of gold leaf. The gold stuck to the glue, and after a moment, the old man blew on it. The rest of the squares of gold leaf blew to the side, leaving a bold design of flowers, leaves, and trailing tendrils in softly gleaming gold.

There is another house where men sit about in the courtyard carving wood, but carving it like jewelry, for the wood they use is fine-grain, hard, and black. There was a figure of a Hindu-Balinese god I especially wanted, but the price of these sculptures is considerable, and I had to forego it. However, the superiority of these wood carvings to the Balinese heads now known so commonly over the world is instantly apparent. All the carvers in this house were true artists, and their work, in the finest Indian-Balinese tradition, is their pride.

Character of the Dance

Most Balinese dances possess an inner intensity, an interior frenzy, which is revealed to the spectator by quick darting movements of widely opened eyes, by quivering fingers, by swift tramplings of the feet, by sudden transitions from one acute-angled pose to another, by whirring fans and the trembling flowers of headdresses. It is as though the dancers are receiving and transmitting a strange, electrifying force that causes every part of their bodies to vibrate intensely. I know from personal experience that Balinese dances are the most exhausting to perform. The dances of Thailand, Cambodia, Java, and Japan, with exception of the demon, or "possessed" dances, are unstrained and refreshing, soothing, even lulling to the mind and body of the performer. Balinese dances make the artist feel, after performance, as though he had emerged from a state of possession or hypnosis.

Dance Training

I lived in a little bamboo, palm-thatched house in a coconut grove by the sea, near the village of Sanoer on the south coast of Bali. Every morning at eight, Ida Bagoes Rai Nyoman Gria came from the village with two musicians carrying a drum and a gender to teach me the Legong. The Legong is the great classic feminine dance of Bali, and from its style many other feminine dances are derived. The Legong is supposedly descended from the dance of the original heavenly nymphs who brought the dance to earth as a gift of the gods. There were, until recently, a number of stories used as subjects for the Legong dances, but now the tale of the King of Lasem has become the popular favorite, and the others have been consequently neglected. As previously mentioned, each guru teaches his own particular style and dance figures, so that each Legong is different from any other, though all tell the same story and introduce the same characters.

The Legong I was taught tells how the King of Lasem, going to war, takes leave of his weeping Queen, who tries to dissuade him, for she has had a premonition of his death. But he is deaf to her entreaties, goes to woo and bid farewell to the Maiden Lankesari whom he found in the forest. Then the Bird of Ill Omen appears, beating its wings, "blood flowing from its beak," a dire presage for the King.

The Legong represents these characters, one by one, in the most ethereal and delicate manner imaginable—a mere breath of suggestion. The costume and style of dance remain the same. Only by subtle differences in the carriage of the body, the expression of the eyes, the manipulation of the fan, can one guess that the Legong is now possessed by the spirit of the King of Lasem, by his unhappy Queen, by the Maiden Lankesari, or by the Bird of Ill Omen. The Legong is highly symbolic and hieratic dance drama, far, far removed from realism. Legong is therefore the most important feminine dance and the one I most wanted to study. My lessons took place under a palm-thatched roof supported on poles over a beaten mud floor. When the musicians were not playing, the soft wind in the coconut palms and the waves splashing the sandy beach continued the melodies of the Legong music.

Ida Bagoes Rai Nyoman Gria had been court ballet master to the King of Karagasem. He taught me by dancing a sequence to show me, then by standing facing me while I imitated his movements. When I had memorized them, he stood behind me, following me as I danced, correcting my torso, knee, and head positions, pulling my arms, wrists, elbows, and fingers into proper line. Lastly, I had to dance before him for final correction.

My lessons lasted four to five hours every day. Rest intervals were spent sitting on the mud floor writing notes. Those were happy days of intense concentration in that ideal setting of sun and shade, beautiful vegetation, perfect weather, and peace.

When I went to live in Denpasar again, I continued my lessons with Ida Bagoes, coming by pony cart every morning to Sanoer. Those were lovely drives through the Balinese countryside along shady roads, past rice fields and through little settlements in the jaunty pony cart. One morning my charioteer sat in on my lesson, making himself useful by playing the drum. He was a member of a Balinese orchestra in Denpasar.

In Denpasar I lived in the comfortable and picturesque guesthouse of Mr. Houbolt, a Dutch connoisseur of Balinese art. He found another excellent Legong teacher for me, Bjoman Kaler. Every morning I had my lesson with Ida Bagoes in Sanoer, and every afternoon, another with Bjoman Kaler in Denpasar. Kaler taught me by having me follow his best Legong dancer whom he brought along for the purpose. She must have been about eighteen, a "mature" dancer for Legong, which is usually danced by little girls between the ages of eight and fourteen. At fourteen they customarily marry, and very well, since they are the most beautiful girls of the village, and dance training has given them poise, confidence, and grace. They often marry Balinese princes, but if they marry less highly, after the age of fourteen they may continue to dance if they are specially endowed dancers, and they may also teach.

As I followed Kaler's pupil, he would stand behind me, correcting my positions and movements, humming the music meanwhile. It was remarkable how different Kaler's Legong was from Ida Bagoes'. The style was necessarily the same, but the figures were vastly different. Ida Bagoes' Legong was restrained with postures like the Indian-Balinese paintings and sculptures, classic in feeling. Kaler's was freer, with extravagant postures and movements, more sensual.

Each group of dancers in Bali has its own individual choreography so that every Legong, every Baris, every Djanger is different from every other, although all have the same basic forms that distinguish them from other dances. To clarify the point, one may consider Western ballet companies: they may each perform mazurkas, czardas, and minuets, and each with individual choreography, yet each mazurka, each czardas, each minuet must have the characteristic steps and figures that mark it as such a type of dance. Or take an example familiar to the general public: ballroom dances. Each waltzing, tangoing or fox-trotting couple may dance with an individual style, yet the basic steps and figures that distinguish a waltz, a tango, or a fox-trot must be there.

Costume for the Dance

The costume for the Legong is one of the most splendid imaginable. Its silks of vivid colors, harmoniously combined, are painted in lavish patterns of curling leaves, flowers, and tendrils in pure gold leaf. The leather ornaments, cut into delicate, lacy patterns, are also painted in gold leaf. The gold-painted leather crown is covered with little white flowers, each trembling on a tiny spring. The gold-leaf-decorated fan, fluttering in the dancer's hand, adds the final touch to the effect of fabuluous richness. The gold-leaf decoration is known as prada work.

The complete costume consists of the following articles:

A long-sleeved jacket, the sleeves decorated with prada.

A prada-embellished kain (a length of material from the armpits to the ankles, and about two yards long, worn wrapped around the body as a skirt).

A torso band, also decorated with prada, about 5 inches wide and 3 yards

long, worn tightly wrapped about the torso from armpits to the hips.
A hip ornament of gold leather, hanging behind.
An apron of gold leather, hanging in front.
A bolero of gold leather.
A collar of gold leather.
A headdress-crown of gold leather and flowers.
Earplugs and armlets.

The headdress has two sprays of white (sometimes of beaten gold) flowers that stand erect just above the temples. The crown of the headdress is covered by little white flowers, each on an individual spring. These flowers tremble constantly, giving a living quality to the headdress and enhancing the intensely vibrant character of the dance.

Color combinations may be: emerald green, magenta, purple, and gold; cerise, yellow, deep blue, and gold; or some similar range of colors. The costume belonging to the author has purple sleeves, purple kain, and a cerise torso band, and all the leather ornaments are backed by green silk which is visible through the lacy perforations.

Masks and Makeup

Many and varied are the masks of Bali, but they are used only in the dramas: Topeng plays, Wayang-Wong, Gamboeh, Tjoepak, and the Barong-Tjalonarang and Barong-Rangda plays. The dances—the Djanger, Kebiyar, Sangyang, Redjang, Kris, Djoged, Maboeang, Mendet, and Legong —use no masks at all, except for the boy who plays the part of the Bird of Ill Omen in the Legong, who sometimes wears a bird mask.

Balinese dancers shave their eyebrows into defined shapes. Their faces are powdered white, eyebrows painted black, and lips red. Their necks, hands, and feet are left their natural bronze color. A round white dot is painted between the eyebrows for feminine dances, and, for Legong, sometimes a white dot at each temple is added.

Makeup for masculine dances is essentially the same. Some masculine roles require masks.

The hair is carefully dressed and pinned up, or, for Djanger and Djoged, frangipani flowers are strung, each on a single hair, giving the effect of a cascade of flowers over the hair, which hangs down the dancer's back. Men and boy dancers in Kebiyar, Djanger, and Djoged wear chic turbans of gold-painted (prada) silk, with a great hibiscus flower over the left ear. For Legong, the dancer's hair is rolled up.

Dance Properties

The only property used in these dances is a Balinese fan of silk with gold-leaf decoration (prada work) like that on the Legong, Kebiyar, Sang-yang and Djoged costumes. Again, the boy who plays the Bird of Ill Omen in Legong uses leather wings, but more often the Legongs themselves represent the Bird of Ill Omen with their fans used like fluttering wings. This is more in keeping with the ethereal, unrealistic spirit of Legong drama than are the realistic painted-leather wings, which must be a modern invention for audiences of tourists.

Music for the Dance

While listening to a gamelan in Bali, S. M. Milevitch, my pianist-composer, exclaimed: "A thousand variations, and with only a five-note scale!" He was enraptured, as have been many other musicians. Indeed, several distinguished Western musicians, upon visiting Bali, have dedicated themselves to the study of Balinese music. The variety of effects that Balinese inventiveness has devised within a five-note scale limit, and with only percussion instruments, is astonishing. Variations of rhythm, accent, pianissimo, fortissimo, diminuendo, crescendo, abrupt stops, muted effects, and bell-like tinklings contrasting with deep gongs, are ever fascinating, ever fresh and new, seemingly flowing from an inexhaustible source of delights for the ear.

There are several five-note scales, each for a traditional use; and various types of gamelans, or groups of instruments, for the various types of plays and dances. The names of those most often encountered are:

gender wayang: for Wayang Kulit (shadow play)

gender wayang ramayana: for Wayang Wong plays

gamelan anklung: composed of very small instruments of ancient type

gamelan selending: of holy iron, and ancient, to accompany ceremonial dances, offerings, exorcisms, and libations

gamelan soeara (voice gamelan): accompanies exorcistical, ecstatic, or trance dances like Ketjak and Sangyang.

gamelan pelegongan: for Legong dances.

gamelan djoged: for Djoged dances.

gamelans for Topeng: for Ardja plays, Djanger dances.

gong kebiyar: the full Balinese "symphony" orchestra which also accompanies Kebiyar dances.

Dances and Performances

There is always something happening in Bali, some dance or ceremony, temple feast or cremation. Usually these affairs last all night. When the Balinese find time to sleep is a mystery. They work all day and play all night. I do not know when I found time to sleep, either, during my stay in Bali. Mornings I studied until noon, then wrote dance notes and practiced, bathed and lunched. Afternoons, evenings, and nights there was always something to see that must not be missed. The very first evening, after our all-day trip from Gilimanoeck, I saw a Djanger.

The Djanger has evolved from much older dance forms, the Ketjak and the Sangyang, both ecstatic trance-dances, but the Djanger shows its former religious connection now only in the offerings made at the beginning of its performance. Djanger is always given in square formation: two lines of boys facing each other and two lines of girls facing each other, forming the four sides of the square. Songs and dances alternate.

In the Djanger, that first night, boys and girls from ten to twenty years old took part. The boys wore European shirts and shorts, bow ties, black-rimmed spectacles, and painted moustaches. Seeing Balinese interpret Europeans makes one conscious that European actors interpreting Orientals must be equally ridiculous to Orientals. The girls wore sarongs, torsos tightly bound with long, gold-painted bands, and the spraying, arched Djanger headdress. This lovely coiffure is similar to the Balinese wedding crown. The boys and girls sat on mats forming the customary hollow square, six to a side, the boys facing one another and the girls facing one another. The Djanger gamelan was ranged behind them.

The form of modern Djanger is said to have been inspired by the visit, some thirty years ago, of a Malay theatre troupe whose repertoire was a potpourri of ideas they had picked up from various ports they had visited. The Balinese could never be accused of lacking imagination or the faculty of adapting what they so readily and wittily observe. In Djanger they found a great opportunity for combining the most contrasting and incongruous elements. The boys make football pyramids, and do acrobatic stunts in the middle of the hollow square; the girls make lovely weaving patterns with arms, hands, necks, and eyes, sitting in their two rows; or, alternating with the boys, dance duos, trios, or solos in the center of the square. At intervals, hair-raising yells from the boys punctuate the dance, accompanied by fierce, swift dartings of their roundly opened eyes. With menacing hand gestures and shuddering bodies, all the boys look to the right, to the left, to the right again. They yell again and repeat the movements. The gamelan bronzes crash and sustain their sonorous ringing. While the Djanger is the least interesting of Balinese dances, it is amusing. This seems to be its sole purpose; it is a social game, and it does have truly Balinese rhythms pulsating through it. It is impossible for the Balinese to do anything without rhythm. The girls always dance serenely, with impassive faces, in "classic" Balinese style. It is the boys who go wild, incorporate ideas snatched from anywhere: cinema (there was one cinema in Bali), a stray magazine, a newspaper picture, the doings of tourists. Every Djanger group has its own variations, always done within the basic frame of a hollow square.

At Sanoer, some days later, Katharine and Jacques Mershon invited me to see a Djanger in their garden, given by children from five to eight years of age. It was convulsingly amusing to watch these tiny creatures executing the dance figures, ogling with their eyes, twitching wrists, jerking elbows and shoulders, fluttering fingers, their little bodies possessed by a vibrant intensity, their faces set in deadly earnest.

The big hotel held special shows for their tourists in the hotel garden, and I was always graciously invited. For these performances, the hotel engaged the best dancers and actors and the most famous gamelan. The guests sat in comfortable chairs on the lawn in the pleasant evening air, and the programs always started more or less on time. Punctuality was a considerable difficulty and a source of worry for the hotel, since the performers sometimes came from distant villages, and a heavy rain might make the road impassable, or some other mishap might occur. The programs were composed of selected parts or shortened versions of musical compositions, plays, and dances, so that the tourists might get a general idea of several types of Balinese entertainments in one evening. Tourists usually could not stay more than two or three days before having to go back to their ship. It required considerable tact and foresight on the part of the hotel to organize such a program, get all the artists there on time, made up and presented in orderly fashion. The hotel's idea of a condensed show was a good, practical Dutch idea, but precisely because of the cuttings, selections, timing, and rush (from the Balinese viewpoint), the artists did not play with the same spirit and self-dedication that they did in their own performances. Very likely they felt they were being "mechanized," made to "prostitute" their art, and at any rate to present it in a hashed-up form to foreign eyes who could not understand it as a Balinese audience would. There was a Balinese audience, however—a row of brown faces watching over the hedges.

The gong kebiyar is the full Balinese "symphony" orchestra, the most beautiful and complicated of all Bali's beautiful music. The dance that is sometimes presented with it is also called Kebiyar and is a fairly recent creation of the Balinese dance genius, Mario. I saw a truly beautiful Kebiyar danced by a pupil of Mario one night. His whirring fan, his quivering fingers, his elegant wrist turnings and flowing arm movements, his torso undulations and seductive eye movements as he sat cross-legged in the center of the hollow square formed by the gamelan instruments, garbed in silks lavishly decorated with gold leaf—all this translated the delicacy, passions, and infinite nuances of the exquisite music into visible form. There is an astonishing figure in the Kebiyar when the dancer, sitting cross-legged, suddenly "hops" across the dancing space with his long gold-leaf painted train sweeping behind. The engotan, the characteristic neck movement that transports the head from side to side, is also used in Kebiyar, which employs an even greater repertoire of eye movements than any other Balinese dance I witnessed. Eyes flash, droop, dart, flutter, melt into a seductive swoon, become fiercely passionate in an endless variety of emotions expressed through the eyes harmonizing with the moods of the music. There was a delightful part in the dance of Mario's pupil when he seemed fascinated and lured by the music. He approached an instrument, dancing, watched attentively, then took the mallets from the musician, and played, himself, with great elegance and delicate flourishes. The Kebiyar, always a masculine solo, gives the impression of the utmost refinement in dance. As we watched this scene by torchlight, my neighbor murmured *"Quelle élégance!"*

One morning there was to be a big dance program in the forecourt of a temple on a country road midway between Sanoer and Denpasar. I put off my morning Legong lesson to drive in a pony cart to the scene, where I arrived early enough to visit the dancers in their dressing quarters in one of the rear courts of the temple. On straw mats behind a curtain they were leisurely dressing. No necessity for quick change troubled them. From baskets they unpacked crumpled costumes and headdresses, straightened them and hung them up. How they ever manage to make those rumpled costumes, kept in baskets since the last performance, look so superb and fresh, is a miracle. They bound each other's torsos with long bands of silks spangled with prada, decorated each other's hair with frangipani flowers by threading each blossom on a single hair. They shaved each other's eyebrows, and painted each other's faces. Like European artists, they did not welcome an intruder into their dressing room, and definitely cold-shouldered me so I did not stay long, but joined the audience under the great waringen tree and waited for the show to begin.

In the shade of the holy tree, on the beaten earth, the first dance took place. It was a Djanger, but more refined and developed than any I had seen heretofore. The girls were exquisitely costumed. This was followed by a scene in Ardja style, played by the famous old actor Ida Bagoes. He walked about, exclaiming, posturing, gesticulating, bowing to the ground with a sweeping movement of his open arms. He seemed to be announcing the coming of someone very beautiful. Then the gamelan began the Tjondong melody for the opening dance of the Legong. The Tjondong had been kneeling before the gamelan with her back to the audience, thus indicating she was invisible, until the instant she rose and turned her face to the audience. Ida Bagoes now retired inconspicuously from the scene. The Tjondong began her dance with gestures of opening a curtain and stepping forth. Her dance was one of wide, sweeping curves carried by rapidly trampling feet across the dancing space, under the aerial roots of the waringen tree. Her eyes darted and flashed, her fan fluttered and beat the air like a wasp's wings. There were tense, angular flexations of elbows and wrists, her knees were in deep *plié*, and her feet beat the earth in rapid little steps similar to a ballet *bourrée*. At the end of each sweeping curve, the feet rose to the highest half-toe possible and the knees straightened; then dropping to the full foot, knees in deep *plié*, the Tjondong darted off again in the opposite direction to repeat the rise to half-toe and the ecstatic pose at the end of the next sweeping curve. The sweeping curves were interspersed with postures when the Tjondong stood still, or walked with carefully placed, slow steps, fanning herself with a most seductive drooping of the eyelids, or at times lolling her head in a way expressive of the greatest suffering, or again, with the fan held as a wing, she trampled the earth with heavy, ominous, and slow steps, eyes staring straight forward as she represented the Bird of Ill Omen. The Tjondong's dance synthesized thus the story of the Legong and introduced the two little girl Legongs who must have been about twelve years old. They were dressed in costumes stiff with gold leaf, and wore gilded head-dresses alive with trembling flowers. These two Legongs, who represent one in double, danced in a style identical to the Tjondong whose costume was also similar to the costumes of the Legongs. But the Legongs' dance was longer, and being a duet, there were more figures. They faced each other, seemed to rub noses and cheeks caressingly—a love scene—and circled, rubbing gently against each other. Sometimes they clasped each other, their heads drooping, their bodies seemingly shaken by great sobs, or one would weep and the other console her. Sometimes their movements duplicated each other's, sometimes they were opposed. With rapid *bourrées* they would dart apart, one right, one left; then, coming together again, they would dance in unison. Now a boy, dressed in Legong costume with two wings on his arms, entered the dancing space, hopping in *plié*, sitting on his heels. He was the Bird of Ill Omen. The wings beat frantically as he pursued the Legongs. They were frightened and tried to beat the Bird off. The Bird hopped in circles about them, striking them with his wings. Something terrible seemed about to happen. After some moments of frenzied dancing, the dancers walked off and the music ceased playing. The Legong was suddenly over.

The Sangyang, a dance of little girls or boys in a trance, is associated artistically with Legong. The Sangyangs are supposed to possess mediumistic powers, and although they have never had dance lessons or learned the Legong, when in a trance they are said to dance the Legong perfectly. They wear Legong costumes. The Sangyang is a purely exorcistic trance-dance.

A most beautiful religious ceremonial dance is the Redjang. In its extremely slow rhythms, sash play, profile figures, management of the train between the feet, slow turnings of the wrists, and leaning into space, it has the dreamy, unworldly quality of the Javanese court dances, the Serimpi and Bedoyo. The Redjang is performed to cast out illnesses, and is therefore exorcistical. It is danced by women.

It was full moon, and there was to be a great temple ceremony. All day preparations had been going on: processions of offerings piled high in colorful pyramids, carried on women's heads, passed by; decorations were placed, and priestly rituals were enacted. In the late afternoon when we arrived, the temple courtyard looked like a three-ring circus. There was so much to see and so much was going on that one did not know where to look first. All around were little shrines with lights and offerings; a gamelan was playing for a group of dancing youngsters. The Bale Poerwa, a holy structure, stood off center, and the great Barong Keket, supported on a wooden bar nearby, waited to be animated for its part in the festival. All these points of interest were filled in with groups of Balinese and their children, a small audience, withall, for so much elaborate preparation. But the festival, like all Balinese festivals, was not given for show, but simply for its own sake.

The Barong Keket is a fantastic animal, more suggestive perhaps of a lion than anything else. Could there be a common, distant origin for the Balinese Barong, the Japanese Jishi (lion) dances, the Chinese lion-dogs that guard Buddhist temple entrances, and the mythical lion-dogs that guard Buddhist temples in Cambodia, Thailand, Burma, and Tibet? The

Barong in Bali is a holy animal, and Barong plays are always given in temple courts. The Japanese Jishi dances have some sacred association, the Jishi mask being considered to represent a sacred animal. I believe the ancient link between these mythical lions may be found in Buddhism, or perhaps much earlier.

Barong Keket has a long, sagging body covered with long, thick, white fur or hair. He is covered with splendid trappings of gilded leather studded with little mirrors or bits of glass, white or colored. His tail, erect and curving like a plume, is also of gilded leather with various ornaments at the end including a little tinkling bell. His face is a lovable-looking animal mask, painted red and polished. He has round, staring eyes, elaborate gold eyebrows, dilated nostrils, and two rows of white teeth that chatter and clack his emotions as he dances. His alert little ears point forward. His face is surrounded by elaborate gilded leather ornaments and surmounted by a huge, fantastic crown of the same material, too complicated to describe. From his chin hangs a black beard decorated with fresh frangipani flowers, each strung on a single hair. This beard has magic powers of healing and restoring to normality. The Barong is the protector against Evil. Evil of course cannot be destroyed, it is a part of creation as Good is, but it can be guarded against and warded off by good influences personified by the Barong. This is the theme of the Barong dance drama. Rangda, who plays opposite the Barong, is the symbol, or personification, of Evil.

Now the time had come for the Barong-Rangda drama to begin. The Barong (having become animated by two men, one the front legs and head, the other the hind legs) ambled amiably forward from where he had stood under two white umbrellas. On he went around the temple court, examining everything with the greatest interest, clicking his teeth and wagging his head with pleasure. Children fell back with shrieks of delight as the Barong approached them. He examined the gamelan, stepped back in amazement, cocked his head to listen, pranced and shook himself in rhythm to the music, rubbed against a musician like an affectionate dog, then galloped off to another corner of the court to some new attraction. This play continued for some time, during which we lost all sense of a mask operated by two men. The Barong had become a real and lovable creature to us.

Suddenly an unearthly, raucous, wailing laugh turned all heads toward the temple gate. There stood Rangda clutching the wall with the glittering nails of her spread fingers while with the other hand she held a white cloth, her magic cloth whose touch brings death to mortals. She swayed in a backward curve, raised her arm, and again emitted that bloodcurdling laugh as she swished her cloth down through the air. A dead silence fell over the court. The Barong stood motionless, staring at Rangda. Slowly she descended the stone steps into the court, gesticulating with her glittering claws, tottering, swaying, emitting terrifying hollow sounds like a mad creature escaped from a grave, for Rangda is Queen of the Graveyard. She swished her dread scarf in various directions—everyone dodged and fled. She leaned precariously, shaking with hollow laughter, her eyes starting from their sockets, her white teeth and tusks gleaming, her long red tongue with golden flames lolling, her long white hair rumpled and disheveled. Her flaccid breasts were two bags of sand that swung and drooped with her movements. Slowly this ghastly apparition advanced toward and circled the Barong, who seemed paralyzed with fear. He crouched, moving tentatively this way and that as though seeking an escape; then, snorting and shuffling, with chattering teeth, he retreated, eyeing Rangda like a bull about to charge, pawing the ground. Then he charged. Rangda struck with her cloth; Barong dodged and swerved. The great combat was on! How long it lasted is impossible to say—all sense of time was lost in the fearsome conflict. Rangda seemed disdainfully mocking and sure of herself. Then it appeared that the Barong was in great danger. Now the kris dancers, devotees of the Barong, rushed forward to attack Rangda, but she flicked them with her magic cloth, and her power turned their rage against themselves. They staggered and reeled and turned, pressing their krises into their own bodies in an agony of mad frustration. But men and priests were watching, and when the frenzy had gone far enough, they seized the kris dancers one by one, disarmed them, and carried them, already numb, in trance, to one side, where they were brought back to normal state in due time. The Barong, now safe, was also in a psychic state. Rangda, temporarily defeated but still triumphant, retired from the scene, disappearing up the steps and through the temple gate by which she had entered, with a last disdainful gesture of her scarf and a lingering, jeering, hollow laugh.

The kris dance was actually no dance at all, only a ritual frenzy of disordered movements. Rangda and Barong always act in the same patterns and style, but with complete individual freedom for improvisation. A parallel might be the Spanish bullfight which is also an ordered ritual, yet each bullfight is different from the others depending on the strength and caprice of the bull and the art and ability of the toreador. I was told that the man who plays Rangda is especially exorcised so that the spirit of Rangda will not possess him permanently, but will leave after the drama is over. It is of course essential that the Rangda-spirit possess him during the play.

The Barong-Rangda drama was followed by a dance of offerings. Torches had been lit long before, and now old priests and priestesses began a stately dance, carrying offerings in a circle around the Bale Poerwa, a little pavilion raised on long poles and serving as a sort of shrine or holy-of-holies, containing offerings and perhaps sacred objects. We saw the dancers as black silhouettes as they passed between the torches and us; then as dimly lit bronze figures when the light fell upon their brown bodies. Some carried flowers; some, food; and some, fire, the flames licking from the vessels. The priests wore only loincloths; the priestesses wore simple kains about their legs, their white hair loose and flowing. Their dance was a Mendet, a "dance of offerings," beautiful in its simplicity, dignity, and purpose. We watched until two in the morning, but activities in the temple court were still in progress as we walked home in the brightness of the full moon.

IMPORTANT BALINESE DANCES

Feminine	Masculine
Legong	Baris
Sangyang	Ketjak
Redjang	Ritual Baris
Maboeang	Maboeang
Djanger	Djanger
Mendet	Mendet
Djoged	Djoged
	Combat dances
	Kebiyar

Dance Technique

Head: Chin slightly lowered and head tilted slightly right or left. The engotan, a sideways jerking of the head, the face always remaining front, is used to mark the end of a phrase. The jerks must coordinate perfectly with the musical accents and timing.

Hands: Left hand: fingers extended, stretched, rigid, quivering. Right hand: open, like Indian pataka, fingers curled softly.

Arms: Extended straight, or bent in sharp angles. The movement pulls from the spine to manipulate the arms. Changes from one pose to another are sharp and swift. Sharp movements of the wrists mark the

musical accents. A snakelike rippling of the arms and shoulders is sometimes used.

Torso carriage: The torso is carried erect, spine slightly arched.

Knees: Deeply flexed throughout the dance except at the ends of phrases
when they are straightened in a pose of upward-reaching ecstasy on
feet in half-toe position.

Feet: Rapid little steps beat the ground in a shuffling, sideways movement
(a Balinese version of a ballet *bourrée*). Slow, carefully placed walking
steps with lifted toes. Elegant poses with one foot full on the ground,
the other in ballet third-position half-toe.

Eyes: Sharp glances from a high point at right side to center front, repeated
without drooping the eyelids or blinking.
Same movement also executed to the left.
Drooping, seductive glances usually accompany slow walking steps.
A fiery, intense expression is used for exciting parts.
A straightforward, round-eyed stare accompanies finishing poses.

Finishing pose (used at end of dance phrases):
Step forward on the left foot, bringing the right foot to back of left
ankle; *plié* deeply on left leg. At the same time bring arms from open
position at sides, together down in front.
Step back on right foot; place both feet in first position, *plié*. At same
time, bring right arm to right side, hand in pataka, and left arm fully
extended to left side from shoulder. Left fingers vibrate. Neck executes
engotan.

Dance Exercises

No exercises were taught, only practice of the postures and movements listed under Dance Technique.

Concluding Thoughts

The Balinese are immensely sorry for anyone who has had the misfortune to be born outside of Bali, and therefore is unable to live in Bali
as his rightful home.

Life in Bali is devoid of mechanization, artificiality, and social problems.
Everything and everyone has his place and fills it with smiling grace. Life
seems utterly natural, balanced, full of interesting activity, joyous—the
way life ought to be—the way it was, perhaps, in the mythical Golden
Age of the world. Bali has been called, with justice, the "Last Paradise."

Back view of Legong costume. The Legong
dance starts with the dancer kneeling before
the gamelan instruments. With her back
turned to the audience, she is "invisible."

The Bird of Evil Omen.

Foot positions. Note gold-leaf work on silk.

Xenia Zarina in the Balinese dance, Legong.
Posture of the King of Lasem. (*photo by Semo, Mexico*)

Xenia Zarina in Legong.
Posture of the Queen mourning. (*photo by Semo, Mexico*)

Djanger performed by children at Sanoer, Bali.

Djanger dancers.

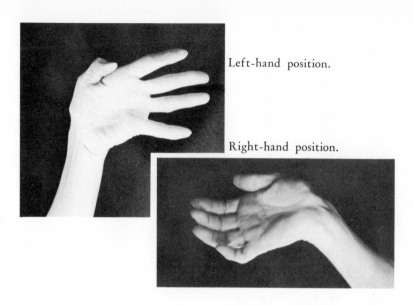

Left-hand position.

Right-hand position.

Legong dancers near Denpasar, Bali.
Note their knee positions, left hands, and shadows.

S. M. Milevitch taking down the music of the Legong at Sanoer, Bali.
Ida Bagoes Rai Nyoman Gria in Legong pose behind musicians.

Legong dancers, one weeping, the other consoling, performing near
Denpasar, Bali. Note gamelan in background under waringen tree.

Closeup of Legong dancer's headdress.

Ida Bagoes Rai Nyoman Gria in the beginning pose of the Legong, the "opening
of the curtain," Sanoer, Bali.

Bjoman   Kaler,   Legong   dance
teacher at Denpasar, Bali.

Ida Bagoes Rai Nyoman Gria in the finishing pose of Legong at Sanoer, Bali.

"Split" temple gate, typical of Balinese temple architecture.

The author in her bamboo house in Sanoer, Bali.

Rangda,
the Spirit of Evil.

Garuda, the mythical
eagle in a dance drama.

Legong dancer with kris.

Balinese dancers.

Balinese dancers dressing for a performance.

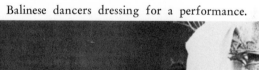

Kebiyar dancer.

Kebiyar danced by a child.

Manner of holding a fan.

Japanese Classic Dance: Nihon Buyo

History of Nihon Buyo

THE HISTORY of the Japanese dance begins with the legend of a divine dance: Amaterasu Omikami, the Sun Goddess, source of light and life, became angered and hid herself away in a cave. The other gods, left in the cold and darkness, foresaw the inevitable result of such conditions; so, uniting their spiritual power in a dance before the celestial cave, they entreated the Sun Goddess to reveal herself and shed her benevolence upon the world again. Thus the world was saved by a dance, for without the sun there can be no life.

The classical dance of Japan traces its evolution for two thousand six hundred years, through the Kagura, Gigaku, Bugaku, Dengaku, folk dances and Noh dance dramas whose elements have been absorbed and blended into what is called today Nihon Buyo, literally, "Japanese Dance," the dance form presented in the Kabuki Theatre.

THE KAGURA

The Kagura, oldest of Japanese dances, is said to be descended directly from the dance of the Eight Thousand Gods before Amaterasu Omikami Sama's cave. The name Kagura means "music in the presence of the gods."

It is a dramatization of historical events, and is to be seen today at Shinto shrines throughout Japan. It is performed as part of the ceremonies for the coronation of a new emperor, and each year a certain day in December is set apart for a Kagura performance in the Tokyo palace of the Emperor. It is danced in the presence of the Emperor and Empress, who are dressed in ancient style suitable to their positions as Chief Priest and Priestess. This performance is a dance prayer for peace and prosperity for all Japan. The Kagura I saw was at Kasuga shrine in Nara, the ancient capital of Japan. It was a religious dance of great charm and interest danced by Shinto priestesses in red-and-white kimonos of ancient style, their sleek black hair hanging down their backs, tied at the nape of their necks by red and silver ornaments, their serene foreheads surmounted by purple flowers. It was a slow and stately dance divided into several parts by the use of ritual objects held in the hands, among which an instrument composed of little bells was most attractive, adding a new element to the music of koto and flute and drums which were played by other priestesses and priests.

In the Imperial Sanctuary, a dance called Mikagura, having reference to the celestial cave episode, is performed on special occasions. Among the people, many Kagura of simplified form are danced for successful crops, for overcoming sickness, for safe return from war, for other social or community needs.

From remote times, a hereditary line of court dancers, called Sarume-no-kimi, have been dedicated to dancing the Kagura. The Goddess of the Dance is considered their ancestress.

GIGAKU

In A.D. 610 the Gigaku was introduced into Japan from Korea. It was a dance drama of supposed Central Asian origin, connected with Buddhist ceremonies. It was danced with masks, and some of the ancient masks have been preserved. They are of fantastic expressiveness, and are guarded as national treasures. There are ten Gigaku dance dramas remaining to us. The Gigaku dances were accompanied by simple music of fife, small drums, and cymbals.

Owing to its association with Buddhist ceremonies, the Gigaku was highly esteemed. The Imperial Court encouraged the art by establishing, in those days, an Actors School to train dancers, thus recognizing the dance as a veritable profession.

Bugaku

In the sixth century, dances from India and China were introduced through Korea into Japan, and were received with great interest at the Imperial Court. These dances, called Bugaku, were much more developed in choreography and in musical accompaniment than Gigaku. They were still, like Gigaku, very simple and elegant in movement, of slow, ritual gestures. They were later incorporated into Buddhist services, and were also presented as entertainment on gala occasions at the houses of nobles. Bugaku is still performed today under the name Gagaku. Even as early as the sixth century, there was a government bureau supervising all dance and music. It was called Gagaku-Ryo, and its ancient regulations give us interesting information.

During the ninth century, the great dancers and musicians of the Heian period collected, classified, and Japanized these imported dances and their music until they attained the form in which they are preserved today at the Imperial Court, and where they are executed at certain seasons by official dancing masters. The costumes are rich in color and design, and the masks in which these dances are presented are fantastic in expression and of wonderful workmanship. Many of ancient date are treasures of the Imperial Museum.

Mai Dances

Purely Japanese and of antique origin are the Mai dances. The Hayato-no-mai, Gosechi-no-mai, Kume-mai, and others which were in existence before the seventh century are still performed on great occasions such as the New Year Banquet, national festivals, and annual fetes of celebrated shrines. Kagura is of the Mai type of dance. Mai dances are always slow and dignified with studied beauty of movement.

Dengaku

In contrast to the aristocratic and refined dances referred to above, a boisterous, comic, acrobatic dance of peasant origin called Dengaku was evolved in the twelfth century. Ancient magico-religious peasant dances performed as offerings to the God of Harvest, to pray for a plentiful harvest and to exorcise evil, were the sources of Dengaku, which became a popular amusement for the people with the addition of juggling, acrobatics, and even dramatic elements. Although of remote origin, the earliest mention of it appears in documents of the late Heian period. We learn from these that not only the dancers but also the spectators went into wild ecstasies. The dance was accompanied by pipes and tambours playing simple, impelling rhythms, and its crude boisterousness appealed to the people, giving them an emotional outlet. Dengaku caused the rise of a new profession: Dengaku Hoshi, who were priests specializing in the performance of Dengaku.

FOLK DANCES

From the earliest times there have persisted among the people old Shinto dances, undoubtedly totemic, performed to invoke good harvest, rain, favorable spiritual influences for the tribal group, and allied desiderata. These dances represent animals, and are danced with masks. The best known are the Boar mask, Cock mask, Dragon mask, Ta Mai, Horse mask, Heron mask, Deer mask, and the famous Lion mask dances. Of course the lion is not indigenous to Japan, but the lion mask was introduced from China through Korea to Japan, and becoming exceptionally popular, was superimposed on the original Deer mask dance. These dances may all be seen at the present time in various regions of Japan, but only at certain seasons. Even on the Kabuki stage one may see famous Kabuki actors perform artistic adaptations of the Lion mask dances called: Kagami-Jishi, Kurama-Jishi, Echigo-Jishi, etcetera.

In rural districts at certain seasons one may see numerous colorful folk dances such as Bon Odori, which is danced during the Festival for the Dead; the Harvest dance; and the Catch Fish dance. The names of these dances and the seasons at which they are danced would indicate that they are descended from very old magic dances which were performed to invoke beneficent spirits. Later they perhaps became part of early religious ceremonies, but now are simply rural amusement dances whose original significance is almost forgotten.

THE NOH DANCE

After the civil wars of the fourteenth and fifteenth centuries, the arts, which had suffered great neglect, were revived again and developed new forms. Inheriting the traditions of Kagura, Mai, Gigaku, Bugaku, and Dengaku, a new and highly stylized form of dance, called Noh, evolved from the hands of two geniuses, Kwan-Ami and Se-Ami, father and son. Noh is the artistic consummation and perfection of all the ancient aristocratic dances. The stern Samurai attitude toward life and death, and the deep spiritual values of Zen Buddhism, which was the religious philosophy of the warrior class, naturally dominated the epoch. The qualities of the warrior philosophy were clearly reflected through Noh, which became the official entertainment of the Samurai class.

This form of dance drama is imbued with a haunting, mystic spirit. It seems not of this world, but transports the observer to eerie regions of discarnate beings. The movements are so slow and so controlled that the effect is hallucinatory. It is as though occult forces activate the actor-dancers. Noh is presented today only in Noh theatres, specially designed and built for the unique requirements of this type of dance drama. The stage floor is of highly polished wood; the background is of wide pine planks whose natural grain is also polished. On them is painted a large pine tree. This is the only scenery used in Noh. A wooden bridge at the audience's left, with a low polished wooden rail, serves as entrance for the actors. A group of musicians sit onstage at the audience's right. The actors wear masks, and the costumes are of magnificent antique brocades.

A typical Noh might begin with the musicians playing a nostalgic melody with flute and drum, or plucking the string of an antique bow (which is used in Noh to call the spirit of a deceased person to manifest itself). After an appropriate lapse of time, the actor impersonating the spirit invoked appears, moving slowly along the bridge as though floating in the air. On reaching the column where the bridge joins the stage, the actor grasps the column delicately, leaning with fixed attention toward the music as though making a great effort to remember something in his past; then slowly lifting hand and arm in some significant gesture, he advances onto the stage, drawn by the irresistible attraction of the strange music. All the while, he seems to be making an intense and painful effort to materialize—to return to the material world, to manifest himself. This vastly interesting art expression has attracted the attention of celebrated authors, both Japanese and European, and several excellent books on the subject are available.

With the perfection of Noh, Japanese theatre arts were set on a firm foundation.

The Kabuki Dance

By the seventeenth century a prosperous merchant class had risen. They wanted entertainment suitable to their spirit and tastes, so the puppet play and Kabuki evolved to satisfy this need. The Kabuki dance incorporated the dance traditions of the past with the characteristics of Ningo-Shibai (puppet play) and Noh technique to form the magnificent Kabuki dance, Shosagoto, the great classic dance of Japan that we see today. Shosagoto is dance drama performed to chanted music whose chief accompaniment is the samisen.

The Kabuki dance was originated by a young vestal virgin of Izumo Shrine, called Izumo-no-Okuni, who became famous for her dances. About 1600, in a temporary theatre in a dry riverbed on the outskirts of Kyoto, she began dancing, and rapidly attained such popularity that the authorities feared for the effect on public morals. A few years later, by order of the Shogun, women were banned from playing in theatres. From then until the present day, male actors exclusively have occupied the Kabuki stage, and have developed a technique for interpreting women's roles with a delicacy and exquisiteness that few actresses can equal and none can surpass. The actors in the Noh theatre are also exclusively men.

Thus we trace Japanese dance from its divine origin through its religious forms: Kagura, Shinto, and Buddhist dances; its court forms: Bugaku and Mikagura; its popular folk-dance forms: secular Kagura, Dengaku, totemic dances, and rural amusement dances; finally, to its great art forms of Noh and Kabuki dances. Each form had its origin in religion, and evolved special characteristics which fitted it to the spiritual requirements of a certain class of society: refined and dignified dances for the Imperial Court; simple, boisterous dances for the common people; impersonal, mystic Noh for the introspective Samurai; and Kabuki, brilliant summing up of all that had gone before, for the new bourgeois class which was to become the core of the social structure of modern Japan.

National Characteristics in Dance

The differences in the dance techniques of each land are determined by the habits of living, climate, clothing, and so forth, but most of all by the spiritual outlook of the people. As the spirit, tastes, and temperament of a people are revealed through their arts, let us see how these qualities are revealed in the Japanese dance.

The Japanese character is formed mainly by a blending of Shintoism, Confucianism, and Buddhism. Shinto, the indigenous and ancient religion, teaches a highly evolved form of nature-worship and reverence for ancestors. Buddhism, teaching the doctrine of the Indwelling Spirit, the Divine Essence in plant, animal, and man, and the Unity of all Life, created a great wave of artistic expression, a great need to make visible to all, the wonderful pulsing of life and rhythm that flows through all things. Kung Fu-tzu (Latinized to Confucius) had a passionate love for music, and held the belief that an understanding of music is essential to good government, a belief shared by Plato and other Greek thinkers. "It is impossible for a vicious man to be a good musician" is one of Confucius' sayings. He insisted on the cultivation of aesthetics, teaching that "Beauty in small things as well as in great should be the formula for life." The actual practice of this maxim is apparent in many phases of Japanese life, and the welding of these three religions is undoubtedly responsible for shaping the Japanese character with its great love of nature and its ability to translate nature into art forms.

The Japanese people have a passionate love of nature and an appreciation of beauty embodied in simplicity and quietude which show in every phase of their life: in their gardens, in architecture, in decoration, in clothing, in religious services, in all the arts, and in daily life. The use of natural woods, polished to show the beauty of the grain in decoration and in architecture; the simple, economical cut of the graceful kimonos; the reserved simplicity of home furnishings; the selection of three, five, seven, or nine perfect flowers for a floral arrangement; the choice of a single pine branch and a moon, or a few reeds and a dragonfly, for a painting; the attention given to the sonorous vibration of a single string in music. These, to cite only a few examples, indicate the restraint of good taste, appreciation of simplicity, and sensitiveness to the Inner Spirit pervading all things. This Indwelling Spirit can be revealed only by suggestion, and is perceived through careful selection of outward signs of its existence. Ability for such selection is a characteristic quality of Japanese mentality.

So it is that in the Japanese dance we find that the principal characteristics are: simplicity; economy of movement (each movement exists for a purpose, and has a definite meaning to contribute to the whole); a highly developed symbolism in the gestures; beauty in line and posture; harmonious sequence; restraint of expression; impersonality, or the suppression of one's own personal feelings the better to reveal the Inner Spirit pervading the dance.

Themes of Dances

TOBAE (THE MOUSE)

A man sets a trap for a mouse that has been making away with food. When he comes home, the mouse is in the trap. It is a lovely lady mouse that pleads with him eloquently, telling him by her dance that she needs food for her children. The man, touched with compassion, frees her, dances with her, and gives her more food to take home. I saw this dance at the Kabuki-Za. It made high comedy of the man's perplexity and the mouse's cajolery and coquetry to win her freedom.

FUJI-MUSUME (WISTERIA MAIDEN)

Part I. Wisteria Maiden enters carrying a branch of wisteria on her shoulder. It is the month of flowers, May, and Fuji-Musume, just twenty years of age, is a symbol of spring and the flowering of young womanhood. She dances her admiration of the pendulous wisteria (turieda) overhead and her joy in the beauty of nature.

Part II. Fuji-Musume dances with a fan which symbolizes now an oar of a boat, now buds opening into flowers, now the rudder of a boat, now Mount Fuji, and so on. These symbols occur as the song indicates and are interspersed among purely decorative dance movements and manipulations of the fan.

Part III. Fuji-Musume, after rearranging her kimono, dances with gaiety and playfulness, manipulating the long sleeves of her kimono, to tell us of her frolic with her sweetheart. The sun is now setting, she takes again the branch of wisteria, and in the final pose, watches the flight of birds across the sunset sky.

THE PRIEST, THE WOMAN, AND THE HUSBAND

A comedy by one dancer with three masks. The dancer changes the masks and head covering instantaneously while turning his back to the audience, to accord with the song the dance illustrates. The dancer's body seems to change shape with the change of mask and action, the costume remaining the same. The woman is a fat little country woman who is trying to flirt with the priest. The priest is slender and dignified. The husband is burly and irate.

SAGI-MUSUME (HERON MAID)

Sagi-Musume appears, dressed in white, in a snow scene. She carries a large umbrella, wears geta (wooden platform shoes) on her feet, and a cloth covering her hair to protect it from falling snowflakes that drift down over the stage. This dance has seven parts, each in a kimono of a different color. It is a feast for the eyes as Sagi-Musume lets fall one kimono at the end of each part to reveal another, more sumptuous, beneath it. At the end of the dance, she resumes her white kimono and flies away as a heron. In the seven parts, she dances with various properties: the large snow umbrella, tenegui (scarf), a bamboo pole with two pails, and a willow branch. It is a dance of tender melancholy, wistful loneliness, snow, and cold. The dance lasts about half an hour.

Musume-Dojoji (Maiden of Dojoji)

Once a young girl fell madly in love with a priest who passed through her town on his return to the monastery of Dojoji Temple. Despite his discouragements, she followed him relentlessly. At last he reached a river and crossed it in the only boat, hurried to the temple, and hid himself under the great bell. The girl, frustrated at the riverbank, became transformed into a serpent, in which form she swam the river, and coiled about the great bell in an effort to embrace her beloved, but the heat of her passion suffocated the priest under the bell.

The dance, Musume-Dojoji, begins here: Long after these events, the spirit of the young girl is reborn as a princess. One day, passing Dojoji Temple, she feels strangely attracted to it. Unconscious of the past tragedy and her part in it, she enters the temple precincts wonderingly. The entrance of Musume-Dojoji is performed in Noh style, showing she is possessed by an irresistible attraction but is unable to understand the strange force that impels her. In the courtyard of the temple, she finds Buddhist priests sitting, and dances for them a series of gay and lovely dances to entertain them.

Musume-Dojoji, in its entirety, lasts an hour and twenty minutes; but any of the dances can be presented as a separate and complete divertissement. Musume-Dojoji is a spectacular entertainment with changes of kimonos and dance properties. The most famous part is Furidasi-no-Dan, the dance with seven red-silk kasa which represent flowers. Furidasi-no-Dan is an evocation of the beauty of flowers. Another attractive part is the dance with suzudaiko (little Japanese tambourines) in gay and complicated rhythms which usually concludes Musume-Dojoji.

Chobei

The most soul-wrenching moment I ever experienced in any theatre occurred during *Chobei,* a historical play. In feudal times when the military classes were oppressing the citizens of Japan, Chobei organized the civilians of his locality to protect their rights and lives against abuses. Chobei was subsequently "liquidated" by the military authorities. The play takes the story up when Chobei receives an invitation to the house of the local lord.

Chobei's wife dresses him in his best for this visit. Hardly a word is exchanged between them during this scene, but both show plainly their inner fear that these are their last moments together on earth. The wife dresses Chobei with the utmost tenderness and repressed grief. With slow, caressing movements she pleats his wide Japanese trousers, stroking them gently down his thighs, turns her face away, and presses her head against him. Chobei, meanwhile inwardly torn, pretends not to notice. Finally the time has come to go, and both, afraid to give voice to their terrible premonitions, thus to weaken each other's fortitude, bid farewell in the normal way, however, with immense tenderness. Chobei comes out on the porch where his little son runs up, clasps his knees, and cries: "Oh, Papa, when are you coming back?" Chobei stands facing the audience, his hands on his son's shoulders. Across his motionless face pass wave after wave of his thoughts and feelings: love for his little son and wife; concern for his fellow citizens, desire to live and protect them all; his lifework, his grief, his fear, his hope that perhaps this visit will come out all right after all; his submission to the inevitable. Then, not to cause his child distress and terror, he rallies his courage, gives the child an assuring caress, a little laugh, and strides down the hanamichi . . . to the fatal visit. How long that moment of reflection, with his hands on his child's shoulders, lasted, I do not know . . . perhaps a few seconds, perhaps an eternity. Before such moments of spiritual power, time loses its value. But this I do know: as Chobei strode down the hanamichi, the whole audience burst into tears. My own, now, after years, still flow at the remembrance of that scene.

NINGYO SHIBAI DANCES

In these, the dancer appears as a doll with sticks attached to the arms. A koken, a man dressed all in black, represents the puppeteer, and manipulates the doll-dancer by the sticks, finally putting the doll away in a box, or carrying "it" off the stage.

Dance Education and Schools

Japan is the "Land of the Dance" par excellence. Nowhere else in the world can one see so much and such high-quality dancing. Dance training has a definite place in education, dance schools flourish, and their annual recitals present large numbers of pupils who have attained the heights of perfection. So excellent are they, and so superbly presented in costumes and stage settings, that the foreign visitor is at first unaware that he is not witnessing a professional performance. I did not realize that I was attending a pupils' recital until the appearance of a tiny mite who could not have been more than five years old. This wee creature, painted and costumed to look like an exquisite old print, maneuvered the heavy robes, manipulated the dance accessories, and mimed so artfully that the entire audience chuckled with glee at the adorable posturings of the baby-artist.

In the course of the last three centuries, many famous dance schools have been established, each one differing subtly from the others, although they all teach the same classic dances accompanied by the same classic music. Of the numerous schools teaching Nihon Buyo the oldest is Sugiyama, founded in 1716. Its successors, Fujima and Nishikawa, date from 1781, and all three survive today. It is principally from the Fujima school that the Kabuki actors are drawn at the present time. The Nishikawa school tends toward the Noh style, teaching a very simple, refined technique. Other schools, such as Hanayagi, Wakayagi, and Bando, specialize in the training of women artists who, when they become proficient and graduate, become geishas. "Geisha" means a highly trained woman artist. The geishas in Tokyo have their own theatre, a sumptuous building in classic Japanese architectural style, where they present all the classic plays, dances, songs, and music. All the performers are women.

The traditions of each school descend through its pupils. When the master considers a pupil has become perfected, he may accord the pupil the right to add the school name to his own, thus forming a hereditary line for the school. The honor of bearing the school name is naturally great, and the custom would seem to maintain high standards and to instill pupils with a feeling of pride and desire for attainment.

Besides studying in an established school, one may of course study privately with a teacher. In my own case, I had the privilege of studying with Matsumoto Koshiro, one of the great Kabuki actors. He had taught Anna Pavlova and her company some years earlier, and Ruth St. Denis and Ted Shawn with their company when they visited Japan about 1926. The Kokusai Bunka Shinkokai (Japanese Cultural Relations Society) made an appointment for me to visit Koshiro in his dressing room at the Kabuki-Za. When we arrived, he was still on the stage, so we sat on cushions on the tatami (straw matting covering the floor) in the spacious dressing room and waited. It was quiet and we could hear the music and theatre sounds from the stage above. There was time to observe the room and its contents. It was like the living room of a Japanese house except for the dressing table. In the tokonomo (niche for displaying beautiful things) hung a scroll painting of a winter scene. A bronze vase stood below it holding an arrangement of pine branches and a single camellia, for it was the winter season. A hibachi, a large bronze vessel filled with sand, had sticks of charcoal burning and a bubbling teakettle on it. Choice Japanese tea-things stood beside it on a tray on the floor. The dressing table, a low wooden table on which were the bowls, brushes, pots, and bottles needed for Japanese makeup, had a full-length mirror. A cushion on the tatami before the mirror was where the actor sat.

Suddenly the quiet was broken. Servants ran in and lined up on either side of the door. Then in strode Matsumoto Koshiro, magnificent in splendid silks and brocades, his face painted elaborately with red streaks. As he exclaimed, "Oh, it was so hot under those lights, I could hardly bear it," the servants rapidly divested him of the complicated layers of sumptuous materials and slipped a simple house-kimono over his shoulders.

Then Koshiro came forward and greeted me cordially. I had brought Ted Shawn's *Gods Who Dance* with me, and now showed Koshiro the photographs and pages devoted to him. He was extremely pleased and gave that little laugh accompanied by a sideways inclination of the head that was characteristic of him. Matsumoto Koshiro spoke some English, and although he had had little practice for many years, what he said was almost faultless. He always spoke English with a shy smile. Now his son rose from beside the hibachi where he had been preparing tea, and brought it to us. Koshiro presented his son, also an actor but trained in the tradition of Danjuro, another great actor-family, whose name he carries. The tea was the ceremonial green tea looking like thick spinach soup and with a fine aroma. It was served in heavy pottery cups, each one individual in color and decoration. These had been made by hand by one of Koshiro's relatives, and were prized for their artistic value. After the tea, Koshiro invited me to sit on a cushion beside his dressing table while he made up so that I might learn Japanese theatre makeup. Then he dressed in Japanese women's kimonos to show me the correct way of putting them on, crossing and tying so they would stay in place while dancing. Through the Kokusai Bunka Shinkokai, Koshiro knew that I wanted to study Nihon Buyo, so he generously said he would make arrangements for me. Every day I was to go to his home and study until he had to leave for the theatre, after which I could remain and work with one of his pupils for "two, three . . . four hours. . . . Don't worry, you will get a lot of dance," he said, smiling. It was time for Koshiro to dress for his next appearance, so we departed, I floating on pink clouds.

At the appointed time, Matsumoto Koshiro's car called for me at the Imperial Hotel where I lived, and took me to his home on the other side of Tokyo. Through the wide gate on which was a brass plate bearing the name of Koshiro's father, Kayemon Fujima, we drove up a wide gravel path to the door of a typical Japanese house set in a big garden. Koshiro received me and surprised me by speaking excellent English—even better than at the theatre! I had brought my dancing accessories with me—kimonos, an obi (sash), tabi (white cloth socks that fit the feet like gloves), and fans. Koshiro now warmed my kimonos over the hibachi, and put them on me with gentle attention.

The living room had sliding doors of glass on two sides which looked out onto the garden. The third side was the tokonomo with a hanging scroll of a winter scene and an arrangement of pine and lilies in a vase below it. The fourth wall was of paper-covered sliding panels (shoji) which opened onto an alcove with a polished wood floor where we were to dance.

O-Chio-San, Koshiro's wife and assistant, now came in. She was a round-faced, smiling girl who, I think, must be the ideal of Japanese womanhood, so patient and gentle, attentive and gracious she was. She went to infinite pains and resorted to ingenious devices to explain points to me; to me, who had only a few Japanese words and she with only a few more of English. The Japanese race is highly endowed with ingenuity, but O-Chio-San deserves full honors for her adroitness in finding ways to explain artistic and philosophic subtleties to a foreigner with so little language in common.

My lessons started with learning Fuji-Musume (Wisteria Maiden). I was taught phrase by phrase. Koshiro danced and I watched. Then he danced and I followed. Then I danced those phrases alone and he corrected me. At three o'clock he had to leave for the Kabuki-Za. O-Chio-San and I went to the front door, knelt and bowed as Matsumoto Koshiro passed through the door, got into the car, and drove away. O-Chio-San and I continued to work until six—about five hours study for me, stopping only to take notes and drink some welcome hot tea, for in winter Japanese houses are unheated except for hibachis. At six I returned to the Imperial Hotel where I worked by myself on my lessons until late into the night. How difficult, how inaccessible that first Japanese dance lesson seemed to

me! But how fascinating! This fascination continued and increased as time
went on and the lessons became easier. I was completely absorbed in them.
I recall one evening when I was practicing a rhythmically intricate part of
Asazuma. Feeling I had at last made some progress, I looked at my clock. It
was five o'clock in the morning. Every day, five days a week, this was my
program of study. I learned Fuji-Musume, the Furitsuzume part of
Asazuma, O-Hara-Me (a boy's dance) and the beautiful Furidasi-no-Dan
part of Musume-Dojoji.

One day at my lesson, Koshiro-sama told me that the next day was
the thirteenth anniversary of his father's death, and there would be a
memorial reception and dinner at the Imperial Hotel. Would I like to
attend? At the appointed time, I went to the large reception hall. There
were a great many people assembled, all Japanese except me; all the great
Kabuki actors, famous geishas who had been pupils of Koshiro, relatives
and friends, all dressed in black. Each, as he arrived, was given a white
flower which he placed in a bowl below a large portrait of Kayemon
Fujima, Koshiro's father. Then, with a low bow before the portrait and
another to the family standing at one side, he took his place among the
guests. When I arrived, I did not understand the procedure, and felt embarrassed over not executing this gracious rite smoothly, but Koshiro-sama
and his family smiled kindly and signaled me to stand with them. Later,
when we went into the banquet hall, Koshiro seated me at the family table
at his left. His son Somegoro, whom I had met in the theatre dressing room
and at Koshiro's home, and who had come to see my dance programs, sat
opposite me. He had a charming face and about as many words of English
as I had of Japanese. We smiled and smiled at each other, both saying how
sorry we were not to speak each other's language. "Sumimasen, sumimasen!"
("I am sorry, I am sorry!") I was introduced to several of the great actors
whom I had seen playing at the Kabuki-Za. Kikugoro, famous for his
women's dance roles, was a tall, strongly built man in his fifties, with a
handsome, pleasant face. Everyone was smiling and cheerful, gathered in
friendship to pay tribute to the memory of a revered actor.

Matsumoto Koshiro's generosity and hospitality were inexhaustible.
Even the car that came to call for me, that I had assumed was his own,
was a private taxi he had engaged for me. I did not discover this until the
end of my studies. I felt considerably embarrassed for all the trouble and
expense I must have caused, especially as he would not let me pay for my
lessons. To top all this, he ordered a beautiful wig for me, made by the

Kabuki wigmakers, with changes of ornaments to suit the dances I had learned. When I first saw the wig, it was being carried in through Koshiro's dressing-room door, mounted on a little wooden platform, by the wigmakers who then tried it on me, sitting before Koshiro's dressing table while he stood watching and smilingly said, "Beauty." This katsura (wig) Koshiro presented to me as a parting gift.

Shortly before I was to leave Japan, I went to Osaka where my beloved teacher was then playing in the Osaka Kabuki-Za during that month. Every day I went to the theatre to watch him act, to visit him in his dressing room, and to take a few more precious lessons in his dressing room when he was not onstage. There was an event of unique interest taking place in the Kabuki-Za. As already mentioned, Kabuki actors are exclusively men. This is a tradition of several hundred years. But this month, in the Osaka Kabuki-Za, a girl was appearing on the stage with the men actors! She was the daughter of Japan's late great actor, Danjuro. Every day when she was dressed to go on the stage, this beautiful young girl would come to Koshiro-sama's dressing room, kneel, and bow her head to the floor in the classic manner to announce that she was ready, for she was acting with him and held him in the greatest reverence.

After the theatre, Koshiro always took me in his car back to the hotel where we were both staying. Koshiro-sama had the Japanese suite— a perfect little Japanese house—on the top floor. The last evening before sailing I went to bid him farewell. He was sitting on the tatami beside a low table. After some tea and conversation, he began looking in a book. Time passed and he appeared so absorbed I thought he must have forgotten my presence. I watched his gentle figure and kindly face bent over the book. He had the face of a saint, and indeed his whole life had been spent in helping others. His charity had taken many forms. Finally he turned toward me with that tender smile and said: "I wish you good navigation, and may you be healthy."

All that time he had been patiently seeking the correct words to express his farewell. It was too much for me. I remembered Chobei and his other brilliant roles, I remembered his infinite kindness and generosity to me—I burst into tears. My beloved teacher, Matsumoto Koshiro-sama!

It was with greatest regret that I learned of the passing of Matsumoto Koshiro at the age of eighty-one, in the winter of 1949. It is painful also to know that his beautiful home and garden were destroyed in the bombing of Tokyo. The Kabuki Theatre was also destroyed, but has been rebuilt.

FAMOUS DANCE SCHOOLS

Sugiyama (Tokyo)	Inoye (Kyoto)
Nishikawa (Nagoya)	Ichikawa (Edo, now Tokyo)
Fujima (Tokyo)	Nakamura (Kyoto)
Hanayagi (Tokyo)	Azuma (Kyoto)
Bando (Tokyo)	Ichiyama (Kyoto)
Wakayagi (Tokyo)	Mizuki (Kyoto)
Umemoto (Kyoto)	Kashiwagi (Kyoto)

Costume for the Dance

Costumes for Nihon Buyo are as varied and lavish as Japanese genius can make them. The Japanese are masters of design and color, and their imagination has no limits. For theatre costumes, there is great scope restrained only by a delicate sense of appropriateness, as, for example, a costume for Wisteria Maiden should have suggestions of wisteria in its color and design; the costume for Musume-Dojoji should have the suggestion or representation of flowers painted or embroidered upon it. Besides being so free artistically, the Japanese are also the most conservative people, with deep respect, even reverence, for traditions. And so we find that the costume for the Kagura, the most ancient Shinto dance, worn by the Shinto priestesses who dance it or play the accompanying music, is of ancient cut, and always red and white, and the costumes for the fourteenth-century Noh dramas and dances are also of the traditional cut and materials similar to those of the epoch.

Three kimonos are basic for Nihon Buyo. The first is a short red silk kimono falling to just below the hips. Over this is bound a red-silk skirt, laid in pleats around the waist. This gives freedom of leg movement and keeps the legs covered. Now comes a red silk brocade kimono with a white silk collar and long, ceremonial sleeves, also bound on firmly about the waist after pulling the collar down behind, about 4 or 5 inches below the base of the neck. Collars worn up against the neck look terribly "countrified" and destroy the chic and grace of which the kimono has so much when properly worn. Now comes the last garment, the elaborate outer kimono, the showpiece, distinctive of the dance to be presented. This usually has a heavy, padded bottom edge—sometimes three pads of variously colored silks appearing like three more kimonos. This outer kimono is put on very carefully, adjusted first to the exact amount that is to remain on the floor (about 18 inches), then folded over the two edges so that the beautiful lining shows, and also the red silk brocade underkimono. All kimonos are folded left over right, like Western men's clothes. Only the burial kimonos of the dead are folded right over left, like Western women's garments.

When donning the kimono, adjust the lower part of the outer kimono and bind it firmly about the waist. Adjust the upper part by putting on the sleeves and folding the sleeves of the red brocade kimono neatly into them. Adjust the collar of the outer kimono to the collar of the red brocade kimono, pulling it well down behind. Bind firmly about the waist, folding any extra length. These outer kimonos are very long to allow for the 18 inches on the floor and the adjustment at the waistline. Now the obi-holder is bound on very tightly. Theatre obis are in two parts: one that wraps around the torso and one that hangs behind. The part that wraps the torso is now tied on; then the part that hangs behind, like a knot with two long strips, is placed on the obi-holder, tied by cords in front; another decorative cord is passed around the center of the obi, tied in front; and the obi-angi, a fine silk scarf, is passed under the obi-holder, under the arms, and tied in a soft knot in front at the top edge of the obi, concluding this elaborate costuming. The beautiful ornamental katsura (theatrical wig) is put on *after* the first short red silk kimono and red skirt are bound on, and of course the feet are already dressed in their white tabi (socks).

Does this seem complicated? Then imagine you are to dance Sagi-Musume (the Heron Maid), who wears *seven* kimonos, one atop the other, and which are dropped one by one during the dance. This is a real costume display! Not to mention the expense of seven gorgeous kimonos plus the underneath ones.

Costumes for Kagami-Jishi (Lion of Kagami), Kurama-Jishi (Lion of Kurama), and Echigo-Jishi (Lion of Echigo) are like a man's clothing or court dress of generations ago: made of gorgeous stiff brocades, shining with interwoven gold threads.

Masks and Makeup

A mask representing a fantastic lion is worn in the above dances. Since there were no lions in ancient Japan, the Japanese conception of what a lion looked like was more fantastic and poetical than actual, and this traditional representation has been continued. One lion-dance (Kagami-Jishi) that I saw in the Kabuki theatre, played by the celebrated Kikugoro

Onoye, began as a lovely lady who turned into a lion. The remarkably fast change of costume into the lion mask and a long reddish-haired wig which was kept flying out in the air during the frantic dance that followed, by extraordinary twistings of the body, head, and neck, was a difficult test of any actor-dancer's abilities.

There are comic dances that use masks, like the one of the man and the lady mouse; or the one of the husband, the wife, and the priest, danced by one dancer who changes masks and mimicry according to the accompanying song. The singing voice also changes tone and quality according to the conversation of the man, woman, and priest.

The Noh plays and Noh Dances also use masks. Noh masks are unique for their beauty of expressiveness, fine craftsmanship, and range of characters, showing many varied emotions. Their finish is highly polished lacquer, and they are true works of art.

Japanese theatre makeup is on a white, water-paint base. Eyes are carefully outlined, eyebrows shaped in black, the mouth is made up full and small in cherry-red, also of water paint. When demons or other fantastic creatures are to be represented, the makeup defies description of its variety and strange effects.

Dance Properties

Of a long list of dance properties—lances, masques, drums, swords, umbrellas, parasols (single, double, and triple), branches of flowers, playthings, scarfs, rods, pails—it is without doubt the fan that plays the most important role. This is due to its artistic and adaptable form whose beauty always attracts, and whose form lends itself readily to represent a wide variety of objects. The manipulation of the fan adds immense fascination and decorative value to the dance. A closed fan may represent the cane of a lame man, a pipe, a sword, the bow of a warrior, an umbrella, a fishing rod. A half-open fan may convert itself into a bottle of sake, a hat, a lantern, a baby, Fuji-san (Mt. Fuji). An open fan may suggest, according to the way it is handled, a plate, a door opening or closing, a boat, a falling leaf, a book, a lotus plant undulating in the water, the rising sun, the setting moon, and so on. The movements of a fan opening and closing may indicate still more things—buds opening into flowers, the fluttering of a bird's wings. There are numerous ways of tossing a fan into the air, giving it curious twists or turns and catching it again in time to the music to add new aerial patterns and brief seconds of exciting loveliness.

Very often the fan is employed for reasons of abstract beauty, to complete the line of the body or the design of the silhouette of the dancer. Indeed, to quote Ted Shawn in his *Gods Who Dance*, ". . . the difficulties Japanese dancers avoid by not having to do acrobatic stunts is more than made up for by the difficulties of the fan-technique. What they do with the fan is almost past belief." The fan is, in fact, the symbol of all the beauty and technical skill of the classic Japanese dance.

Music for Nihon Buyo

Japanese music is a rich and fascinating field almost unexplored by Westerners. Its novelty, original treatments of musical problems, and quite new points of departure that it offers to the development of modern Western music make it eminently worthy of study.

The character of the music is entirely in accordance with other artistic expressions of Japan. As we have already seen, the Japanese have always held a profound reverence for nature; therefore it is not surprising that they have sought to reproduce in music the spirit of music found in nature. They have sensitive appreciation for quality in sound and pitch, and have selected for their music only sounds with musical value. The Japanese love of simplicity leads them to prefer single notes in music rather than the complicated sounds in harmonization, so that the beauty of each tone may be fully appreciated. Count Kiyoshi Kuroda, in an article on Japanese music, expressed the musical concept of his people in these words: "As a race, we never liked to think of tone as something fixed mechanically by reasoning and which would be regarded as inviolable. To our ancestors it was intolerable as well as inconceivable to segregate Man from Nature. They listened with full delight to all things beautiful . . . ecstatic joy they felt in the timbre of the pure and simple notes of Nature."

The national appreciation of quietude, of the beauty and complexity embodied in simplicity, is manifested in Japanese music. It is the harmonization of the quiet, the contemplative, the spiritual. A French friend once said: "People say Oriental music is tiresome? To me, Western music is tiresome (*fatigante*) because it is nearly always dynamic, active, harmonized, so many sounds to listen to all at once, that one becomes quite worn out trying to keep up with it. Oriental music, on the other hand, is restful to the mind and refreshing to the spirit."

Japanese music is homophonic. All the instruments have rich sonority because the beauty of the vibration of a single string is greatly appreciated.

In Noh plays, the string of an ancient bow will be plucked to attract the spirit of a departed person, the twang of a bowstring possessing mystic vibrations that aid the spirit to materialize and converse with the living.

The principal instruments used in Japanese music are:

samisen (3-stringed, long-necked, square sound box, played with an ivory plectrum held in the right hand while the fingers of the left press the strings as in guitar playing)
shakahachi (bamboo vertical flute)
tzuzume (drums)
wood blocks
koto (horizontal harp with 13 silken strings)

Music for the classic dance is principally singing accompanied by one or more samisens, drums, wood blocks, and a shakahachi. The composition usually begins with the shakahachi and wood blocks, the singing voice coming in later. When the atmosphere has been established, the dancer enters, or being already onstage in some pose, begins to dance. While the voice sings, the dancer represents the meaning of the song through movements; when the purely musical intervals (without song) occur, the dance also becomes pure dance, that is, movement for the beauty of movement without dramatic significance, but of course in harmony with the preceding and succeeding dance sequences.

The whole dance drama, which may take anywhere from twenty minutes to more than an hour, is divided into distinct parts. At the conclusion of each part, the dancer takes a pose on the forestage, looks long at the audience, then, shyly turning his back, runs upstage, balancing the head gently from side to side. At the back of the stage, he prepares for the part to follow by rearranging kimonos, head ornaments, and dance properties. The music, during this preparation, continues with perhaps intriguing samisen variations displaying considerable virtuosity, or the song that prepares the audience for the next part, or some other musical device to connect the parts in an artistic and entertaining way. For the next part, the dancer, now ready, turns to face the audience, and dances again. At the conclusion of the dance drama, the dancer takes the final pose while the closing of the curtain is accompanied only by drums and wood blocks, with sometimes the shakahachi giving a fading effect.

Some lovely modern dances have been arranged to the music of the koto. The koto lies horizontally on the floor, and the player kneels beside it and plucks the silken strings with the right hand while the left delicately moves the ivory bridges. Hands playing a harp are always lovely, and no less so, playing the koto. The sonority of the koto is uniquely beautiful, due to the very choice wood used for the sound box, its shape, and the use of silken strings. The polished wood case is often gold-lacquered in exquisite designs, making the koto as lovely to the eye as to the ear.

The koto is traditionally played by blind musicians. The most famous koto-player in Japan when I was there was an elderly blind man.

There is a story of an emperor of olden times whose beloved, Kogen, played the koto to the delight of the court. But the prime minister was jealous of the emperor's love for Kogen, for he wanted the emperor to marry his daughter, so the prime minister slyly exiled the favorite. The emperor, as months passed, became ill with longing for his beloved. Then one of the courtiers, seeing the grief of the emperor, set out secretly to find Kogen and bring her back. He sought all over Japan until, nearly relinquishing hope, he came one evening to a small village in a pine forest. As he passed despondently, he suddenly heard the sound of a koto and recognized its music as a court melody. Thus he found Kogen and restored her to the emperor.

Music for the classic dances has been properly and completely recorded by the Japanese Victor and Columbia companies. Recordings have been made of the finest Kabuki musicians; the sound is properly reproduced, and the records are as excellent as the best Western records. Although Matsumoto Koshiro told me it is not good to dance to records as one's movements then tend to become mechanical, still, in presenting Japanese dances in other lands where Japanese musicians are not available, one cannot do better, inasmuch as these records are perfectly made, and with a good amplifying apparatus, give the impression that real musicians are playing offstage.

Presentation of Nihon Buyo

The stage setting for Nihon Buyo is the most beautiful of all Kabuki scenes, for its purpose is to create an idealized atmosphere. The white wood floor platforms are specially designed to give resonance to the accents of dancing feet. The backdrops are painted with that transparency and perspective characteristic of all Japanese painting; and overhead hang the turieda, or hanging branches of flowers, leaves, or other effects corresponding to the season represented by the dance. The dance costumes are luxurious to the last degree; the colors of the silks and patterns of the embroidery are guided by tradition, but are of a wide variety due to Japanese genius for design and coloring.

The dancer can come onstage in several ways: by the hanamichi (ramp) through the audience; by the karakuri (sliding platforms) or by various other devices. On the hanamichi, the dancer does not ordinarily enter directly onto the stage, but dances what might be termed a "prelude" on the hanamichi itself.

For the Kabuki dance dramas, the musicians are seated in a box platform at the audience's right, or across the back of the stage. They are costumed uniformly in court dress of the Edo period, and make a picturesque addition to the whole scene.

The extent and variety of Nihon Buyo are seemingly inexhaustible. Nothing could be funnier than the comic dances, more poignant than the tragic dances, more exciting than the demon dances, or lovelier than, for example, Sagi-Musume (Heron Maid) or Musume-Dojoji (Maiden of Dojoji). There is also the Ningyo Shibai, the puppet play, with a history of several hundred years. It is one of the sights of Japan. Unquestionably it is the most highly developed puppet theatre in the world. The exquisitely costumed dolls even dance Nihon Buyo. Ningyo Shibai dances are included in the Nihon Buyo repertoire. The dancers act like dolls while another actor takes the part of a puppeteer, operating the "doll" with sticks.

When not presenting flowers, sometimes Japanese audiences present lovely puppet dolls—or some other thoughtful gift—to artists over the footlights. Very often the gift is an envelope containing money but not the name of the donor.

There is a custom in Japan that all artists would hope to see spread worldwide. It is the practice among Japanese business firms, at home and abroad, to support art and encourage artists by buying blocks of tickets to concert programs, and making up parties among their employees and friends for dinner and the theatre.

The Kabuki Theatre

There is an ancient saying: "A king may be judged by the condition of dancing during his reign." And Confucius said that the music of a nation indicates the political state of the government of that nation. In *Gods Who Dance*, Ted Shawn writes: "Where a nation is strong, its dance is in a flourishing condition. When it is weak and declining, conserving its powers, its dancing weakens and degenerates."

In my own travels through many lands, I have found that a survey of the theatres indicates infallibly the state of the national well-being. Where the theatres are dirty, uncared for, the attendance poor and the presentations

unworthy, that country is in a decadent, disorganized, and dangerous condition. Where theatres are attractive, well kept, and well attended, the
national life is healthy, unified, and strong. In no other land of the Far
East is the theatre so prosperous, so cared for, so respected, and so magnificently presented to the public as in Japan. Theatres of all classes—cinema,
revue, drama, concert, recital, and the classic theatres, Noh and Kabuki—
all are modern, well equipped, attractive, and spotlessly clean. All theatres
seemed full all the time, well patronized, and I have seen people standing
in line for theatre tickets at six o'clock in the morning during an earth-
quake!

Because the Kabuki theatre is the great frame, the setting, for the
classic dance, a glance at those features that differ from the European
theatre is appropriate. The stage opening, instead of being high and narrow
like an old-fashioned window, is relatively low and extremely wide, giving a
panorama effect. The Kabuki stage in Tokyo measures over 120 feet in
width. The stage floor is made of white, polished wood platforms, so fitted
together that the divisions are imperceptible. No one is allowed to walk
upon these platforms with ordinary shoes; only Japanese tabi (cloth socks)
may tread thereon. One day I was practicing in brand-new pink satin toe
shoes, but was ordered off! Every technical detail of stage machinery has
been carefully studied, and all is operated by hand, thus ensuring perfect
timing with the dramatic action. The revolving stage, new in the Occident,
and found only in the most advanced theatres, is a Japanese invention,
and has been in use more than two hundred years in the Kabuki-Za, as
have been the sliding platforms called karakuri, and the hanamichi (flowery
way), a raised ramp extending from the stage through the audience to the
back of the auditorium. It is used for actors' entrances or exits in certain
cases. It lies at the audience's left and gives greater amplitude to the action
of the play or dance, as well as establishing an intimate feeling between
stage and audience. A few Western theatres have been equipped in recent
years with sliding platforms, revolving stages, and hanamichi ramps (all
Japanese inventions), which are advertised as the latest and most extraordinary development in Western theatre.

The scenery in the Kabuki-Za is often changed before the public's
very eyes, rapidly, ingeniously, in a most entertaining and artistic manner,
the audience never seeing anything it should not see. Effects to give atmosphere such as snow, falling blossoms, chirping of insects on an autumn
afternoon, or distant howling of dogs on a winter night show acute obser-
vation of life and artistic discretion in its interpretation. The painted
scenery, unlike old-fashioned European scenery which was painted with

gobby, heavy oils, is done in water colors with the transparency of actual atmosphere and real art value as a picture.

The Kabuki-Za in Tokyo is built of natural woods in classic Japanese style. The lobbies and corridors are hung with beautiful paintings, sometimes with exhibits of paintings. The theatre houses several little restaurants where one can eat, during intervals, a light Japanese meal on a lacquer tray. Apart from the entertainment offered on the stage, the theatre building itself and the Japanese audience dressed in kimonos of many colors and patterns are spectacles full of fascination for foreign eyes. The programs are printed in English with librettos of the plays so that foreign visitors may understand the performance. As soon as a foreigner enters the Kabuki-Za lobby, a program in English is cordially proffered.

Highly effective musical accompaniments, especially the musical recitations, are psychologically timed to excite the emotions. The gorgeously costumed actors' art has been perfected through the generations to such refinement and vital accuracy that no other dramatic art can supersede it, and few compare with it. I do not make this statement without appropriate comparison for I have seen Eleanora Duse, Otis Skinner, the English Players, Stanislavsky's Moscow Art Theatre, the Comédie Française, and others of the greatest in Western theatre art.

This is the Kabuki theatre, the setting for the classic Japanese dance, Nihon Buyo.

FAMOUS CLASSIC DANCES OF THE KABUKI THEATRE

Dances representing women	Dances representing men
Fuji-Musume (Wisteria Maiden)	O-Hara-Me
Musume-Dojoji (Maiden of Dojoji)	Benkei
Shio-Kume	Tomo-Yaka
Asazuma	Goro
Sagi-Musume (Heron Maid)	Omatsu-Kyoran-Mago
Sarashi-Ona	(the Drunkard)
Kagami-Jishi (Lion Mask)	Tomomori
Kurama-Jishi (Lion Mask)	Bunya
Echigo-Jishi (Lion Mask)	Komachi-Sakura
Yama-Uba (in Noh style)	Tzuna Yakata (Sword dance)
	Urashima (famous fairy tale)
	Modori-Kaguo (the Pilgrim)
	Sho-Jo (from a Noh play)

Life of a Kabuki Actor

The profession of a Kabuki actor is not always hereditary, but in Matsumoto Koshiro's case it is. His father was Fujima Kayemon, an adored artist of the Fujima school whose name he carried. He was especially noted for his dancing of women's roles. Matsumoto Koshiro's sons are also Kabuki actors. They are Komazo Ichikawa, Somegoro Danjuro, and Shoroku Onoye. Ichikawa, Danjuro, and Onoye are names of historical actors and also the names of schools of acting founded by them.

All the most famous Kabuki actors are men of sixty, seventy, even eighty years of age. I saw one wonderful old actor of eighty who had to play sitting down since his legs were paralyzed. His acting was so clearly defined, so gentle and eloquent, that his playing of the role (a tragic one) moved the spectator profoundly. The performance of the younger actors, contrasted with that of the older actors, brought out strikingly the recompense that age and experience give. Like fine old wine, their acting was mature and rich, charged with spiritual depth and understanding. Theatregoing publics that demand youth rob themselves of artistic greatness.

Matsumoto Koshiro was, I believe, sixty-eight when I studied with him. Every afternoon he went to the theatre where he took part in the various plays and scenes that compose a Kabuki program. The schedule of the Kabuki theatre presents twelve programs a year which run a full month each. Each program is composed of short plays, tragedies and comedies, historical or imaginary, which alternate with dance dramas based on historical incidents, folk themes, and comic, tragic, or poetic fantasies. The Kabuki-Za begins at 3:30 in the afternoon and ends about 11:30 or midnight—eight hours of delight for the theatre lover. Once a year, during the month of November, all the great actors of Japan appear together in the Tokyo Kabuki-Za. The first time I attended the Kabuki-Za was in November, when I had the opportunity of seeing this brilliant spectacle.

The actors have attractive, immaculate, and comfortable dressing rooms with trained attendants to dress and undress them, and to care for the expensive costumes. Friends may call on actors at convenient times. It was constantly interesting to me to sit in Koshiro's dressing room and watch the life backstage. Visitors removed their shoes at the door, as in Japanese houses. What an excellent custom! Formerly it prevailed in many countries, and with the development of modern ideas of hygiene, it is strange that this custom should not be worldwide. Surely, leaving the dust, dirt, and microbes of the street outside the house, and entering clean rooms with feet shod in clean and comfortable house slippers, is an advantage to all. The visitors, just inside the doorway, made the ceremonial bow to the actor, who replied and invited his guests to take places near him. Often the visitors brought something choice to eat, or fine tea, or a useful or amusing object as presents to the actor. These little gifts were always delightfully wrapped and tied. In no other land have I seen such attractive packages as in Japan—ribbons and papers, uniquely folded and tied, each one different and original.

During one of my visits, an admiring friend brought a piece of white silk. That month Koshiro was playing a famous classical role with an elaborate facial makeup. When he returned to the dressingroom and was decostumed by the attendants, he knelt before the mirror, took the piece of white silk, and centered it on his face. Two assistants held it firmly at the sides of his head while Koshiro carefully pressed the silk against his face until the paint came through the silk. When the silk was gently drawn off, there was revealed on the cloth a perfect reproduction of Koshiro's face in this celebrated role. The friend intended to have this length of silk mounted as a kakemono or hanging scroll as an original souvenir of the actor.

Technique of Nihon Buyo

Japanese classic dance is really dance drama built upon the accompanying song whose poetic words are illustrated by gestures. To represent the vast extent of ideas expressed in the song-poems, the dance was obliged to invent a rich repertoire of gestures, subtle and stylized. Appreciation of Nihon Buyo depends in large measure on an understanding of these gestures and of the song-poems.

Nihon Buyo may be divided into three styles: masculine, feminine, and infantile. The movements for the masculine style are large, energetic, virile; those for children's parts are gay, light, carefree and full of childish vitality; those for women are characterized by tenderness, modesty, coquetry, and grace. Of these three styles, it is above all the feminine style which is considered the most difficult, and is the first to be studied. Kabuki actors, being exclusively men, will naturally dance like men, but to dance like women requires study. The foundation of Nihon Buyo is primarily the dancing of women.

There is another classification for Nihon Buyo: Mai, Odori, and Shosa.

Mai is slow, dignified, comparable to adagio. Odori is light, gay, rhythmical, equivalent to allegro. Shosa is dramatic, pantomimic. But the term
"odori" is commonly used to mean the dance in general as, for example:
Nihon no Odori, Japanese Dance.

Plastic balance and beauty of line are sought in Nihon Buyo. Therefore,
the most expressive angle, the diagonal position, is presented to the audience, and is fundamental in all important poses. In the feminine style, the
S line is greatly admired, and its accentuation is achieved by flexation of the
knees, the manner of wearing the kimono well pulled down at the back
of the neck, the line of the obi, and by the heavy, padded edges of the
kimono sweeping the floor. Feminine hands, when not pantomiming, carrying accessories, or engaged in graceful, rhythmical movements, are kept in
the long sleeves. The hands, when displayed, are made to appear more
slender by folding the thumb over onto the palm, the fingers extended
straight and parallel.

In walking or running, the feet glide lightly over the floor, the
dancer carrying a mental image of the thickness of a sheet of paper
separating his feet from the floor. This thought gives lightness to his
movements. In feminine dances, the slightly toed-in position of the feet
is essential to keep the kimono properly in place, and the knees must
always be together. In masculine dances the knees are widely opened and
turned out as in ballet first or second positions. From time to time, to give
accent with the music and contrast in the dance, a light stamp of the foot,
or a series of stamps, is given. An alternate sliding back of the feet in a
rhythmic series of 2-3-4 movements is characteristic.

The Japanese manner of sitting, in the dance as in life, is for women
to sit with legs folded beneath them; men sit with legs crossed.

Head and eyes give expression to and enhance the significance of
gestures. The end of a series of movements or a dance phrase is marked by
a pose ending with two, three, or four movements of the head, just as a
sentence in literature is punctuated. The end of a part, a "chapter" of a
dance, is signified by the dancer's turning his back to the audience and
walking rapidly upstage, that is, to the back of the stage; the head in
feminine roles is meanwhile balanced rhythmically from side to side. This
balancing of the head is an artistic stylization of a natural movement
caused by the weight of the elaborately dressed and decorated hair. At
the back of the stage, in full view of the public, the dancer changes
properties, rearranges the kimono, even taking off or putting on another
kimono, and takes the posture preliminary to the continuation of the

dance. As three kimonos—or even more—are worn, the removal of the outer kimono in full view of the public involves no "striptease" but rather gives opportunity for the display of another beautiful garment. In these preparations, the dancer may be assisted by a koken dressed in black, whose face is covered by a black cloth which thus renders him "invisible" to the audience.

But the greatest power of expression, as well as the most complicated, resides in the hands and fingers. They indicate objects or represent them by two methods: the direct, realistic manner or the indirect, suggestive manner. For example: the moon may be indicated by a circular movement of the hands, lifted, and eyes looking upward; or by a finger pointing toward the heavens, the eyes following the movement. The first is the direct, representational method; the second, the indirect, suggestive. Sleep is indicated by touching the eyes in the realistic way, or by gestures of arranging the futon (Japanese mattress) on the floor and inclining the head toward the hand. A butterfly may be represented by a fluttering of the hands (direct) or by cautious gestures of catching a butterfly so as not to crush its delicate wings (suggestive). There are two ways of counting: by holding up one hand and, with the index finger of the other, pointing out the number on the fingers of the first hand; or by extending the hand, looking at it intently while folding first the thumb, then the fingers, down over the palm. This will count up to five. If six or more are desired, the fingers which are now folded down must be opened again, starting with the little finger which was the last to be folded down.

The long decorative sleeves are often used to aid in the expression of ideas, and Japanese dancers have a great variety of accessories to use in adding interest and decorative value to the dance.

George Bernard Shaw wrote: "Technique can give one style; but it cannot give taste, or good sense, or power, without which style is an affectation and an impertinence." In Nihon Buyo, the spirit is considered more important than elaborate technique. The whole aim of Nihon Buyo is to express the very soul of a personage, or the very essence of a particular time, place, or object represented in the dance, and to do so by naturalness of movement. "Naturalness" does not mean "realism." Japanese dance is too conventionalized and symbolic to be realistic. But it is natural in the sense that none of the movements causes great physical strain, such as do the aerial leaps and tours de force of European classic ballet, or the splits and other contortions of acrobatic dancing. That the movements used in Nihon Buyo are based on nature, are undistorted and unstrained, is evidenced by the fact that the greatest Japanese dancers are often men of great age. No breakneck stunts disfigure the refined conception of natural, unforced beauty and its conventionalization into art form. Throughout runs the exquisite thread of extreme simplicity, and, except in the case of demon dances, where extraordinary feats of activity are most artistically welded into the dance as appropriate to the character, there are no breathtaking tours de force in Nihon Buyo. The very idea of a tour de force, a physical effort used to astonish an audience to gain applause, is revolting to an artistic temperament that responds to a stimulus of spiritual beauty.

Behind the physical side of the technique of Nihon Buyo, there lie a deep spiritual training, concentration, and introspection, which are manifested through, or rather exhaled from, the whole body. In this training, the dance approaches religious training, especially as found in Shinto and Zen Buddhism. The outstanding difference between the Japanese and European conceptions of the dance, and the quality responsible for almost all other differences, is the value placed on the revelation of the Indwelling Spirit. The European ballet places the principal emphasis on perfect technical execution, although it must not be overlooked that great Western artists like Anna Pavlova have always infused their work with a spiritual quality. The degree to which an artist is capable of submerging himself in his role undoubtedly determines his degree of spiritual quality and, consequently, his greatness.

Training to acquire this spiritual power is impossible to explain. It is mainly an unconscious absorption of spiritual power from the master. Japanese art education has hard-and-fast rules, but is based on intuitive methods that develop the pupil's own individuality.

How can one describe this spirit, this feeling with which the Japanese dance must be infused? How can words describe the perfume of a flower to a person who has no sense of smell? How picture the colors of a sunset to the blind? The music of a harp to the deaf? Who can capture the evanescent beauty of the dance and put it into dry words to give a living vision?

As the Chinese say, "One picture is worth ten thousand words"; so to see a dance is worth more than reading volumes about it. And of course the most direct way to understand and appreciate the dance is to study it through actual lessons. Dance lessons are not only the immediate and joyous road to understanding the dance, but give, as nothing else can, that illumination of the spirit, that wonderful inner joy that comes from the union of the body, mind, and spirit.

Dance Exercises

The only exercises are practicing the dances, following the rules noted under Technique of Nihon Buyo.

Concluding Thoughts

That Nihon Buyo will be preserved far into the future seems certain, for the love for it lies deep in Japanese hearts. Everyone seems to know it and understand it. I have already mentioned that many young people and children study it as part of their education.

Numerous small shops are devoted exclusively to dolls of all sizes and materials which represent most of the classic dances. All the big department stores have sections devoted to dolls, many elaborately dressed like the classic dance figures. Some of these dolls are so exquisite that they are mounted in individual glass cases as much as two feet in height; some are so miniature that they must have been made with a magnifying glass. The production of so many dancing-doll figures would indicate a public interest to purchase them, and indeed a doll is a favorite gift in Japan.

Matsumoto Koshiro.

Shinto priestess-dancer at
Kasuga Shrine, Nara.

Shinto priestesses
who dance Kagura at Kasuga Shrine.

Matsumoto Koshiro
at home, Tokyo.

Bell instrument
used in the Kagura.

Matsumoto Koshiro
in his garden, Tokyo.

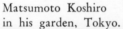

Matsumoto Koshiro
in his dressing room,
Kabuki Theatre, Tokyo.

O-Chio-San with
a samisen.

Xenia Zarina in Musume–Dojoji,
Maiden of the Dojoji Temple. (*photo by Studio Iris, Paris*)

Xenia Zarina
in Musume–Dojoji.
(*photo by Noutiyal,
Mussoorie, India*)

Xenia Zarina
in Musume–Dojoji,
the opening dance
in Noh style.
(*photo by Noutiyal, Mussoorie, India*)

Midori Nishizaki in Echigo-Jishi
(Lion of Echigo).

Midori Nishizaki in Benkei.

Midori Nishizaki in a Lion Dance.

Xenia Zarina as Fuji–Musume,
Wisteria Maiden.

Note fan representing Mount Fuji
in Fuji–Musume.

(photos by Noutiyal, Mussoorie, India)

201

Noh fans:

closed,

open,

forward, back.

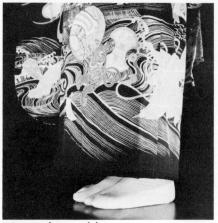
(a) starting position

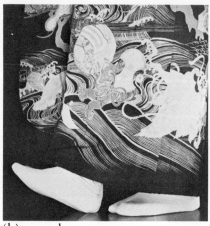
(b) second movement

Noh walk:

(c) third movement

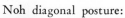
Noh diagonal posture:

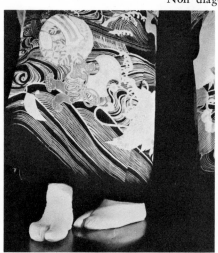
feminine style together

masculine style apart

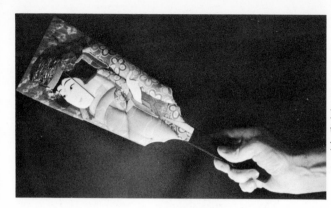

Battledore,
used in certain
youthful play dances.

Kikugoro Onoye
portraying female
in play Kagami–Jishi.

Kikugoro Onoye, celebrated Kabuki actor, dancing Asa-zuma, Kabuki Theatre, Tokyo, with musicians seated traditionally as background.

Kikugoro Onoye transformed into lion in play Kagami-Jishi.

Kikugoro Onoye
performing on the hanamachi.

Japanese doll dressed as a dancer.
Doll and flowers were gifts pre-
sented over the footlights to
Xenia Zarina in Tokyo.

Kikugoro Onoye
dancing Musume-Dojoji,
Kabuki Theatre, Tokyo.

Kikugoro Onoye,
dancing Asazuma.

Matsumoto Koshiro
in a favorite role,
Kabuki Theatre, Tokyo.

Matsumoto Koshiro
in Kabuki plays.

Matsumoto Koshiro in Kabuki play.

Matsumoto Koshiro in Kabuki play.

Matsumoto Koshiro
as Bunya-no-Yasuhide
in the posture-dance Bunya.

Matsumoto Koshiro as
Nippon Daemon in the play
Shiranami Gonin Otoko.

Matsumoto Koshiro
in play Sugawara
Denju Tenarai Kagami.

Yennosuke Ishikawa in play Yumiya Taro.

Scene from dance drama in a Kabuki theatre.

Glossary

Abhinaya—gestures used in Indian drama and dance
Abhinaya Darpana—Sanskrit treatise on gestures used in Indian drama
   and dance
Adaus—sequence of Indian dance steps
Airlangga—Javanese King
Amaterasu Omikami—Japanese Sun Goddess
Angkor—ruins of Khmer civilization
Angkor Thom—city of Angkor
Angkor Vat—temple of Angkor
Anjali—reverential salute (Sanskrit)
Apsaras—celestial dancer
Ardja—Balinese drama
Arjuna—Indian, Javanese, and Balinese hero
Arjunavivaha—Javanese scriptures about Arjuna
Asazuma—Japanese Nihon Buyo dance
Ashtakshara—Indian hymn to Vishnu

Bale Poerwa—holy building in a Balinese temple-court
Baris—Balinese masculine dance
Barong Keket—Balinese fantastic animal, the personification of Good
Batik—Javanese textile
Bayon—temple of Siva in Angkor Thom
Bedoyo—Javanese Court dance (feminine)
Bharat Natyam, Bharat Natya, Bharata Natya—most ancient Indian dance
Bharata Muni—ancient sage of India
Bhatara Guru—Javanese divinity, the Great Teacher
Bhima—invincible warrior, friend of Arjuna
Bird of Evil Omen—character in Legong dance
Bols—Indian dance counts
Bon Odori—Japanese folk dance
Borobodur—Javanese Buddhist monument
Brahma—Indian God of Creation
Bugaku—ancient Japanese masked dance (Buddhist)

Carnatic—of or from South India

Chidambaram—temple to Siva in South India whereon are carved the 108 postures of Siva's Dance of Creation

Chobei—Japanese hero; also a Kabuki drama on Chobei's life

Chulalongkorn—King of Siam (now Thailand)

Chuti—facial paste used for Kathakali makeup

Dalang—storyteller whose voice accompanies dance-dramas in Java and Bali

Delsarte—author of treatise on laws of movement

Dengaku—ancient Japanese dance

Denpasar—capital city of Bali

Deva Dasis—South Indian temple dancers

Devata—celestial being

Djanger—Balinese dance

Djoged—Balinese dance

Djokjakarta—Javanese capital city and seat of Sultan of Djokjakarta

Echigo–Jishi—"Lion of Echigo," Japanese dance

Edo—former name of Tokyo

Engotan—Balinese neck movement

Fête des Eaux—Cambodian celebration on Mekong River

Fuji-Musume—classic Japanese dance

Fujima—Japanese dancing school

Gaekwar Sayaji Rao—Maharajah of Baroda State

Ga-jax-ngo-ling—posture (also called ngla-yang) used in Serimpi and Bedoyo dances

Gagaku-Ryo—ancient Japanese government bureau

Gamelan—Javanese and Balinese groups of musical instruments

Gandharva—celestial musician

Garuda—mythological protector of humanity

Gedruk—Javanese dance step

Geisha—Japanese woman artist

Gigaku—ancient Japanese masked dance (Buddhist)

Golek—Javanese and Balinese marionette

Gopinath—famous teacher and dancer of Kathakali

Gopis—Indian female cowherds, devotees of Lord Krishna

Guru—teacher

Guru Sankaran Nambudripad—famous teacher of Kathakali

Guru-upadesha—that which the Guru taught

Guru Vandanam—salutation to the teacher

Hamangkonbouwana VIII—Sultan of Djokjakarta, Java

Hanamichi—the "flowery way," Japanese theatre ramp to stage

Hanuman—monkey-hero of Ramayana stories

Heian—historical period of Japan

Hotei—Chinese God of Happiness and Prosperity

Ikat—textile made in India, highly valued in Java
Izumo Shrine—Japanese shrine
Izumo-no-Okuni—originator of Kabuki dance

Jinjit—Javanese dance step
Jishi—Japanese lion dance

Kabuki—Type of Japanese theatre
Kabuki-za—Kabuki theatre (sometimes spelled Kabouki)
Kagami-Jishi—Japanese Lion-of-Kagami dance
Kagura—Japanese Shinto dance
Kain—batik cloth used in Java and Bali as a skirt
Kakemono—Japanese scroll painting, hung vertically
Kalakshetra—school of Bharat Natyam in Madras, India
Kalana—Javanese dance (masculine)
Kapang-kapang—Javanese dance step
Karakuri—sliding platforms in Japanese theatres
Kasa—Japanese umbrella, also the property that resembles a little
    umbrella, carried in certain Japanese dances
Kathak—type of dance performed in northern India
Kathakali—type of dance (masculine) performed in southern India
Katsura—Japanese theatrical wig
Kawi—archaic Javanese language, conserved in the classics
Kayemon Fujima—famed actor-dancer, father of Matsumoto Koshiro
Kebiyar—Balinese dance; also Balinese orchestra
Keprak—Javanese wooden sound box used to mark dance rhythms
Ketjak—Balinese dance
Khmer—ancient Cambodian civilization and race
Khon—classic Thai dance form, danced always by men and boys
Kinara—celestial singer (male). Also spelled Kinnara
Kinari—celestial singer (female). Also spelled Kinnari
Kiprah—Javanese dance for men
Kogen—Japanese heroine
Koken—"invisible" assistant on stage, dressed in black
Kokusai Bunka Shinkokai—Japanese Society of Cultural Relations
Koto—Japanese horizontal harp
Kraton—Javanese palace and enclosure
Krida Beksa Wirama—school of dance and music in Djokjakarta, Java
Kris—Javanese and Balinese sword
Krishna—Indian Pastoral God
Kurama-Jishi—Japanese Lion-of-Kurama dance
Kwan-Ami—oroginator of Noh dance

Lakhon—classic Thai dance, danced by women or by both sexes
Lama—Tibetan priest
Lankesari—character in Legong dance
Lasem, King of—character in Legong dance
Lasya—feminine style of Indian dance

Legong—Balinese feminine dance; also a Legong dancer
Leyak—Balinese evil spirit

Maboeang—Balinese dance
Mahabharata—Indian epic poem
Mahout, Henri—French explorer who discovered ruins of Angkor
Mai—Japanese dance style, slow, dignified, graceful
Majapahit—last Javanese Empire before Arab conquest
Malayam—South Indian language
Mangkoe Negoro—Prince of Surakarta (liaison officer)
Manipuri—type of Indian classic dance from Assam, eastern India
Mata-Kelipan—movement of eyes used in Javanese Serimpi and Bedoyo dances
Mataram—eighteenth-century Javanese Empire
Mekala—Lightning Goddess of Thai mythology
Menaka (Lady Sokhey)—famous Indian dancer
Menam—river in Thailand
Mendet—sacred Balinese dance
Mikagura—ancient and sacred Japanese dance
Mkot—golden headdress for Cambodian dancers (also spelled Monkot)
Mongkot—golden headdress crown, used only by royalty in Thailand. A
    dancer's headdress is called "tchedah" in Thailand
Mudras—Indian hand positions
Musume-Dojoji—Japanese classic dance

Nandikesvara—author of the *Abhinaya Darpana*
Nang-Ma-Tcha—Goddess of the river Menam (Thailand)
Nara—ancient capital of Japan
Nataraja—Lord of the Dance, name for Siva in his aspect as Divine Dancer
Nattuvan—teacher of Bharat Natyam
Natya—dramatic dance
Natya Sastra—Sanskrit treatise on dance art
Natya Veda—ancient and sacred book on dance art
Nautch—North Indian term for "dance"
Ngla-yang—posture used in Serimpi and Bedoyo dances (also called ga-
    jax-ngo-ling)
Nihon Buyo—Japanese classic dance
Nihon Odori—light, gay Japanese dances
Ningyo Shibai—Japanese puppet play
Nishikawa—Japanese dancing school
Noh—Japanese thirteenth-century dramas and dances
Nolah-noleh—Javanese head movement in the dance
Nritta—Indian pure dance expressing moods or emotions
Nritya—Indian dance accompanying and illustrating a song

Obi—Japanese woman's sash
Obi-angi—silk scarf worn above the obi
Odori—gay, light Japanese dance
O-Hina San—Japanese girls' festival

Paku Alam—Prince of Djokjakarta (liaison officer)
Panchakshara Mantra—hymn to Siva
Pandji—Javanese hero, friend of Arjuna and Bhima
Panung—length of cloth worn as a woman's skirt in Thailand; also the
    Cambodian male garment
Parvati—goddess, consort of Siva
Patjak-kulu—Javanese head movement in the dance
Patola—rare textile from Gujerat, India, called "ikat" in Java
Pi-Pat—Thai orchestra
Pi-Phat—Cambodian orchestra
Prada—gold-leaf application on silk, much used in Bali
Prambanan—group of Brahmanic ruins in Java

Radha—wife of Lord Krishna in Radha-Krishna stories and dances
Rama—Indian God-Hero; also several kings of Siam (Thailand)
Ramasoun—Thai God of Thunder (associated with Mekala, Lightning Goddess)
Ramayana—Indian epic about Rama
Rangda—Balinese Spirit of Evil
Rasa—Indian word meaning "flavor"
Ravana—wicked king of Ceylon in Ramayana stories; in Thailand and
    Cambodia he is called "Tosakan"
Redjang—Balinese ceremonial dance for women
Ringit Tyang—high Javanese for Wayang Wong (human theatre)

Sadjen—religious ceremony at beginning of Javanese dances
Sagi-Musume—Heron Maid, Japanese classic dance
Sailendra—ancient Javanese dynasty and kings
Samdach Preas Kron—Cambodian genie of the dance
Samisen—Japanese musical instrument
Sampot—Cambodian textile used for women's skirts
Sampour—Javanese dance scarf for men
Samurai—Japanese warrior
Sangyang—Balinese trance dance, similar to Legong in style
Sarumeno-kimi—hereditary line of Japanese court dancers
Se-Ami—originator of Noh dance
Sembah—Javanese reverential salute
Serimpi—Javanese feminine court dance
Shakahachi—Japanese bamboo flute
Shinto Shrines—shrines of ancient Japanese religion
Shogun—Japanese military ruler
Shosa—dramatic, pantomimic Japanese dance
Shosagoto—Japanese classic dance drama
Sita—consort of Indian Hero-God, Rama
Siva—Indian god, Lord of Creation
Siva Nataraj—Siva, Lord of the Dance
Soumping—Javanese ear ornament for the dance
Srikandi—Javanese goddess

Sugiyama—Japanese dancing school
Surakarta—Javanese capital city in Central Java
Susuhunan—Javanese ruler of Surakarta State

Tabi—Japanese foot gloves
Tali—marriage badge given to Deva Dasis on joining the temple
Tandava—Indian type of masculine dance
Tandu—Siva's chief disciple to whom he taught Tandava dance
Tango—Japanese boys' festival
Tatami—Japanese floor matting
Tayoungan—Javanese dance-entrance walk for men
Tchedah—headdress for Thai dances
Tcheou Ta-kouan—Chinese Ambassador to Angkor in the twelfth century
Telugu—South Indian language
Tevada—celestial being (alternative for Devata)
Thais—formerly called Siamese
Tiang—Cambodian and Thai dance platform
Tjondong—first dancer in a Legong dance
Tobae—classic Japanese dance
Tokonomo—niche in a Japanese house for displaying objects of beauty
Topeng—Javanese masked dance-play
Tosakon—Thai and Cambodian name for Ravana
Trance dances—Balinese Sangyang and Ketjak
Travancore—South Indian State
Turieda—overhead borders of hanging flowers in the Kabuki theatre

Utdet—Javanese woman's dance scarf

Vallathol—Indian poet
Vedas—ancient and sacred books written in Sanskrit
Vedic—of or from the Vedas
Vidadaris—heavenly dancers (Javanese mythology)
Vishnu—Indian god

Wayang Golek—Javanese puppet theatre
Wayang Kulit (or Wayang Klitik)—"leather theatre" for shadow play
Wayang Ourang—human theatre (Malay for Wayang Wong)
Wayang Purwa—"ancient theatre," shadow play or human dance-drama
Wayang Topeng—Javanese masked dance-drama
Wayang Wong—Javanese dance-drama, human theatre
Widadaris—heavenly dancers, Javanese mythology

Yaksha—mythological giant, Indian and Thai
Yeak—mythological giant, Cambodian
Yoga—ancient Indian system of physical, mental, and spiritual culture

Bibliography

India

Coomaraswamy, Ananda. *The Mirror of Gesture*. New York: E. Weyhe, 1936.

———. *Fourteen Indian Essays: The Dance of Siva*. New York: Noonday Press, 1957.

Gopinath and Nagabushan. *Abhinayamkuram* (on Kathakali). Madras, 1946.

Goetz, Hermann. *The Art of India*. New York: Crown Publishers, Inc., 1961.

Majmudar, M. R. "The Tradition of Folk Dances in Western India," *Journal of the Indian Society of Oriental Art* (Calcutta), XIV, 1946.

Row, Leela. "Nrtta Manjari, Fundamentals of Bharata Natyam," *Journal of the Indian Society of Oriental Art* (Calcutta), XIV, 1946.

Bhagavad Gita. Mentor Classic. New York: New American Library of World Literature, 1954.

Teachings of the Compassionate Buddha. Mentor Classic. New York: New American Library of World Literature, 1955.

The Upanishads. Mentor Classic. New York: New American Library of World Literature, 1957.

Venkatachalam, G. *Dance in India*. Bombay: Nalanda Publications, 1947.

Thailand

Phra Chen Duriyanga. *Siamese Music*. Bangkok: Department of Fine Arts, n.d.

Tamra Fon Ram (Textbook on Dancing). Text entirely in Thai. Many valuable illustrations. Published as a memorial to a young prince of the royal family. Bangkok, n.d.

Cambodia

Groslier, George. *Danseuses Cambodgiennes.* Paris: Augustin Challamel, 1913.

Grousset, René. *Civilizations of the East.* (4 Vols.) New York: Knopf, 1931–1934.

Cogniat, Raymond. *Danses d'Indochine.* Paris: Editions des Chroniques du Jour, 1932.

Marechal, H. *Guide Archaeologique aux Temples d'Angkor.* Paris et Bruxelles: Editions G. Van Oest, 1928.

Marechal, Sappho. *Costumes et Parures Khmers.* Paris et Bruxelles: Editions G. Van Oest, 1927.

———. *Danses Cambodgiennes:* Saigon: Editions de la Revue Extrême Asie, 1926.

Samdach Chaufea Veang Thiounn. *Danses Cambodgiennes.* Hanoi: Imprimerie d'Extrême Orient, 1930.

Java

Lelyveld, Th.-B. van. *La Danse dans le Théatre Javanais.* Paris: Librairie Floury, 1931.

Bali

Covarrubias, Miguel. *Island of Bali.* New York: Knopf, 1938.

de Zoete, Beryl and Walter Spies. *Dance and Drama in Bali.* London: Faber and Faber, Limited, 1938.

Japan

Akiyama, Kenzo. *History of Nippon.* Tokyo: Kokusai Bunka Shinkokai, 1941.

Kawatake, Shigetoshi. *Development of Japanese Theatre Art.* Tokyo: Kokusai Bunka Shinkokai, 1935.

Miyake, Shutaro. *Kabuki Drama.* Tokyo: Hosokawa Printing Company,

1938, 1948, 1952, 1953, 1954; also Rutland, Vermont: Charles Tuttle Company.

Sugiyama and Fujima. *Outline History of Japanese Dance*. Tokyo, 1937.

Toki, Zemmaro. *Japanese Noh Plays*. Tokyo: Tokyo Toppan Printing Company, 1954; also Rutland, Vermont: Charles Tuttle Company.

Umemoto and Ishizawa. *Introduction to the Classic Dances of Japan*. Tokyo: Sanseido Company, Ltd., 1935.

Other Books

Ellis, Havelock. *The Dance of Life*. Cambridge, Mass.: Houghton Mifflin Company, 1923–1929.

Shawn, Ted. *Gods Who Dance*. New York: Dutton, 1929.

Index

Boldface numbers refer to illustrations